I0605133

To:

From:

Date:

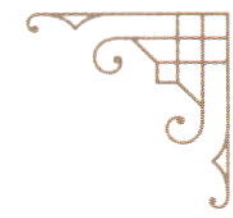

OUR FIRM FOUNDATION

Bible Verses Every Christian Should Know

JOSH MOODY

Christian Art
PUBLISHERS

Visit Christian Art Gifts, Inc., at www.christianartgifts.com.

Bible Verses Every Christian Should Know: For Knowing God and Following God

Published by Christian Art Gifts, Inc., Bloomingdale, IL, USA.

The author is represented by The Steve Laube Agency (stevelaube.com).

First edition 2025

Designed by Christian Art Gifts, Inc.

Cover and interior images used under license from Creative Market.

Most Christian Art titles may be purchased at bulk discounts by churches, nonprofits, and corporations. For more information, please email SpecialMarkets@cagifts.com.

ISBN 978-1-63952-901-8

Printed in China.

30 29 28 27 26 25
10 9 8 7 6 5 4 3 2 1

For Elijah:
that you might know
and love the Bible.

Contents

Note to the Reader:

The power of the Bible is made especially evident in times of exceeding crisis. The Gideon's Bible found in a hotel room, turned to for help when the drugs run dry. The Bible imprinted with words of encouragement from the king, given to the troops entering World War I and World War II. The Word that was a Rock of comfort to David in the cave as he hid from Saul. This Bible, these verses from the Bible, have fed the hungry, shed light on the darkened prison cell, lifted the downcast, given words of praise to the joyful, and directed the lost to paths of blessedness. What greater treasure in the world could there be than the very words of God in written form? What greater use of our time could there be than giving ourselves to recount, and recall these words, so that we might recite in the inner chasms of our mind and heart the very truth of God?

Dear reader, let no delay keep you from the task at hand. Turn to the Bible. Hear His voice—the voice of your Shepherd, the command of your King, the tender word of your good Heavenly Father, the summons to salvation of your Savior, the call to spiritual battle of your Captain. Listen to Him, learn from Him, follow Him.

Josh

How to Use This Bible Verse Guide:

Why are these verses so important?
What makes them essential
for every Christian to know?

Christians must understand important things about God and important things about ourselves if we are to fully enjoy our relationship with God and to actively grow in faith. This book provides a guide to these important topics. Josh Moody draws our attention to 15 aspects of God's character and 15 key elements of Christian practice or discipleship. Together, these 30 reflections help us to know God and to follow Him.

We cannot truly know and follow God without the instruction He has given us in the Bible. For this reason, Josh points us to the Bible verses that help us understand each topic. This little book is like a bright spotlight shining on some of the most treasured Bible passages. It was created to help new followers of Jesus understand Christianity or for long-time Christians to rediscover delight in the bedrock truths of the Bible.

Here are a few tips that will help you make the most of this guide:

- *Select one or two verses to memorize from each topic.* The guide includes lined space for copying the verses or for jotting down key words that help you recall the verse. The passages are also broken into phrases (line divisions) that make memorizing them more intuitive and manageable.

- *Become familiar with all of the verses.* There are more than 270 verses highlighted in this book, so you probably won't memorize all of them. However, you can read them and reflect on them. Perhaps use the note-taking space to jot a prayer or your own thoughts.
- *Read these verses in your own Bible.* You will notice that we've used multiple Bible translations. You can use your own Bible to read and memorize these verses in the translation that you find most helpful or that your church uses. It's also valuable to explore more about these verses by reading the whole paragraph or chapter where they are found.
- *Pause to pray.* God's Word is living and active (Hebrews 4:12). Ask God to use these verses to help you know Him and follow Him. Pray for the encouragement and joy that comes from seeing God's goodness and walking closely with Him.

Knowing God

By faith we understand
that the entire universe was
formed at God's command,
that what we now see
did not come from
anything that can be seen.
Hebrews 11:3 NLT

Knowing God as Creator

In our modern world, we are trained to look at the universe all around us through the eyes of a materialist. It is hard for us who tend to think of things as "nothing but" matter to realize that, even scientifically speaking, things are not so simple. A person of sensitivity and thought, will realize that the age-old question, *Where do we come from?* cannot be brushed aside or shrugged off as a useless question to ask! We feel deep in our bones that we are made for something, and our relational nature indicates more that we are made for Someone. The Bible tells that us that everything that exists has been made by God and is sustained by God. It is true that no human was present at the moment of creation, so we have no firsthand, historical data or scientific textbooks from that time. It is "by faith we understand that the universe was created by the word of God" (Hebrews 11:3). But then, what alternative is there? It also requires faith to believe that this universe is eternal and therefore was never created (a position held by some in the past). And it takes even more faith to believe that something came out of nothing. There must be a beginning and a cause—an ultimate source for everything. In Jesus Christ, we meet that source. Jesus is the Word by whom all was created. We bow before Him as God and worship Him as our Creator.

Genesis 1:1 KJV

In the beginning God created the heaven and the earth.

Genesis 1:27 NLT

So God created human beings in his own image.
In the image of God he created them;
male and female he created them.

Psalm 19:1 ESV

The heavens declare the glory of God,
and the sky above proclaims his handiwork.

Jeremiah 10:12 NLT

But the LORD made the earth by his power,
and he preserves it by his wisdom.
With his own understanding he stretched out the heavens.

John 1:1–3 KJV

In the beginning was the Word,
and the Word was with God,
and the Word was God.
The same was in the beginning with God.
All things were made by him;
and without him was not any thing made that was made.

Colossians 1:16 NIV

For in him all things were created:
things in heaven and on earth, visible and invisible,
whether thrones or powers or rulers or authorities;
all things have been created through him and for him.

Hebrews 1:2 NLT

And now in these final days,
he has spoken to us through his Son.
God promised everything to the Son as an inheritance,
and through the Son he created the universe.

Revelation 4:11 NASB

Worthy are You, our Lord and our God,
to receive glory and honor and power;
for You created all things,
and because of Your will
they existed, and were created.

The LORD has made
the heavens his throne;
from there he rules
over everything.
Psalm 103:19 NLT

Knowing God as Sovereign

When we say God is sovereign, we are saying that He is *the king*. The idea of God as king spans the Scriptures. It is rooted in God's creation of the world (Genesis 1:1) and His rule over it. God's rule as king is represented in the kings of Israel, specifically King David. There was always a plan and a hope that God's rule, His kingship (imperfectly administered through even the most godly of kings) would one day come to real fruition. The beginning of Matthew's gospel paints the picture of Jesus as the king—He is great King David's greater son. Few doctrines are more comforting to the Christian than the truth that God is sovereign. We do not always know the end from the beginning—but He does. We cannot always understand how He will bring good out of evil—but He does. And He has revealed His extraordinary sovereignty at no more surprising a place than the cross of Jesus Christ. Our king is a crucified king. In the book of Revelation, Jesus' scars are revealed as tokens of His compassionate, loving, merciful, and mighty sovereignty. While the friends of God rejoice in His sovereignty, the enemies of God quake before His power. Let all who are wise, then, come on bended knee before King Jesus. He is merciful to repentant sinners. He delights to win a victory over evil and hell through His redemptive work, triumphing over all the powers of darkness. One day His rule will be extended to every corner of our heart and every corner of the entire universe.

Job 42:2 NASB

I know that You can do all things,
And that no plan is impossible for You.

Psalm 93:1 NKJV

The Lord reigns, He is clothed with majesty;
The Lord is clothed, He has girded Himself with strength.
Surely the world is established, so that it cannot be moved.

Proverbs 21:1 NASB

The king's heart is like channels of water
in the hand of the LORD;
He turns it wherever He pleases.

Isaiah 45:5-7 NIV

I am the LORD, and there is no other; apart from me there is no God.
I will strengthen you, though you have not acknowledged me,
so that from the rising of the sun to the place of its setting
people may know there is none besides me. I am the LORD,
and there is no other. I form the light and create darkness,
I bring prosperity and create disaster; I, the LORD, do all these things.

Isaiah 46:9-10 NIV

Remember the former things, those of long ago;
I am God, and there is no other;
I am God, and there is none like me.
I make known the end from the beginning,
from ancient times, what is still to come.
I say, "My purpose will stand,
and I will do all that I please."

Zechariah 14:9 NLT

And the Lord will be king over all the earth.
On that day there will be one Lord—
his name alone will be worshiped.

John 10:27-28 NASB

My sheep listen to My voice, and I know them, and they follow Me;
I give them eternal life, and they will never perish;
and no one will snatch them out of My hand.

Romans 9:18 NLT

So you see, God chooses to show mercy to some,
and he chooses to harden the hearts
of others so they refuse to listen.

In the year of King Uzziah's death
I saw the Lord sitting on a throne,
lofty and exalted, with the train
of His robe filling the temple.
Seraphim were standing above Him,
each having six wings:
with two each covered his face,
and with two each covered his feet,
and with two each flew.
And one called out to another and said,

"Holy, Holy, Holy, is the LORD *of armies.*
The whole earth is full of His glory."

Isaiah 6:1-3 NASB

Knowing God as Holy

To say that God is holy is to say that He is *different, other, set apart, special*—and supremely so. When Moses encountered God in the burning bush, even the ground around the bush was holy because God's holiness emanated out in an awesome field of specialness. When Isaiah saw the vision of God in the temple, he described God not merely as holy but as three times holy. In Hebrew, the superlative is indicated by repetition. To say something is very good you would say something is "good, good." But only God is three times holy! He is holy in a way beyond all human categories. *How are we to know this holy God given that we are sinful, unholy, people?* This is the great question of the Bible. The answer appears finally in the coming of Christ, who is declared also to be holy and whose life and death bridge the gap between us and God. Jesus is the God-man who gave His life to take away the sins of the world. Through repentance and faith, we receive His righteousness, and we become a child of God. We are declared righteous and holy before God our Father. As Christians, this is our status, but it is not yet our daily, practical reality. Practicing holiness needs to be worked out gradually, in the power of the Spirit and through faith. We practice holiness in the middle of a faithful church, in prayer, and in spiritual battle against temptation. One day, we will be fully holy. For now, the battle is on. We repent and trust Christ for fresh power each day to walk in holiness. And at the very start of that process is a recognition of God as holy, holy, holy.

Leviticus 19:1-2 ESV

And the LORD spoke to Moses, saying,
"Speak to all the congregation of the people of Israel
and say to them, You shall be holy,
for I the LORD your God am holy."

1 Samuel 2:2 NASB

There is no one holy like the LORD,
Indeed, there is no one besides You,
Nor is there any rock like our God.

Psalm 99:9 KJV

Exalt the LORD our God,
and worship at his holy hill;
for the LORD our God is holy.

Isaiah 57:15 ESV

For thus says the One who is high and lifted up,
who inhabits eternity, whose name is Holy:
"I dwell in the high and holy place,
and also with him who is of a contrite and lowly spirit,
to revive the spirit of the lowly,
and to revive the heart of the contrite."

2 Corinthians 5:21 NIV

God made him who had no sin to be sin for us,
so that in him we might become the righteousness of God.

Hebrews 12:10 NLT

For our earthly fathers disciplined us for a few years,
doing the best they knew how.
But God's discipline is always good for us,
so that we might share in his holiness.

1 Peter 1:14-16 NIV

As obedient children, do not conform
to the evil desires you had
when you lived in ignorance.
But just as he who called you is holy,
so be holy in all you do; for it is written:
"Be holy, because I am holy."

Revelation 15:4 NLT

Who will not fear you, Lord, and glorify your name?
For you alone are holy.
All nations will come and worship before you,
for your righteous deeds have been revealed.

For God so loved the world,
that He gave His only Son,
so that everyone who
believes in Him
will not perish,
but have eternal life.
John 3:16 NASB

Knowing God as Love

The one thing most people affirm about God is that God is love. Yet, few realize how God's love has far more than merely sentimental implications. In the Bible, the love of God is rooted in the *hesed* or covenant love of God as revealed in the Old Testament. God showed himself as lovingly faithful and steadfast to Moses and to the wayward people. God loved them even though they were unfaithful. Psalm 136 repeats over and over again the remarkable lesson: God's "steadfast love endures forever." But how? Given that God, as we have seen, is not only love but also holy, how can He love sinners without compromising the very nature of who He is, and indeed the moral fabric of the universe? The great question that the Bible seeks to answer is not so much *How can a loving God send people to hell?* but *How can a holy God send anyone to heaven?* The answer lies in that most famous of Bible verses, John 3:16. This verse explains that God's love and justice are jointly revealed at the cross where Jesus gave Himself for us. When we follow this King of Love, King Jesus, we are increasingly remade into His likeness. We become more loving. This is the reason for the famous words of the apostle Paul in 1 Corinthians 13, telling an unloving church (yet proud of its giftedness) that the most important gift is love. Faithfully loving our family and friends and neighbors and even strangers is the greatest reflection of God's love.

Exodus 34:6-7 NIV

And he [God] passed in front of Moses, proclaiming,
"The Lord, the Lord,
the compassionate and gracious God,
slow to anger, abounding in love and faithfulness,
maintaining love to thousands,
and forgiving wickedness, rebellion and sin.
Yet he does not leave the guilty unpunished;
he punishes the children and their children
for the sin of the parents to the third and fourth generation."

Psalm 136:1 ESV

Give thanks to the Lord, for he is good,
for his steadfast love endures forever.

Hosea 11:1 NKJV

When Israel was a child, I loved him,
And out of Egypt I called My son.

Zephaniah 3:17 ESV

The Lord your God is in your midst,
a mighty one who will save;
he will rejoice over you with gladness;
he will quiet you by his love;
he will exult over you with loud singing.

Romans 5:8 NIV

But God demonstrates his own love for us in this:
While we were still sinners, Christ died for us.

Romans 8:38-39 NLT

And I am convinced that nothing
can ever separate us from God's love.
Neither death nor life, neither angels nor demons,
neither our fears for today nor our worries about tomorrow—
not even the powers of hell can separate us from God's love.
No power in the sky above or in the earth below—indeed,
nothing in all creation will ever be able to separate us
from the love of God that is revealed in Christ Jesus our Lord.

1 Corinthians 13:13 ESV

So now faith, hope, and love abide, these three;
but the greatest of these is love.

1 John 4:16 NKJV

And we have known and believed the love that God has for us.
God is love, and he who abides in love abides in God, and God in him.

The steadfast love of
the LORD never ceases;
his mercies never
come to an end;
they are new every morning;
great is your faithfulness.
Lamentations 3:22-23 ESV

Knowing God as Faithful

For God to be faithful is for Him to be true to His character and true to His word. Whatever God promises He will *do*. God is who He is. "There is no variation or shadow due to change" (James 1:17) with God. He is utterly reliable. These truths related to God's faithfulness have comforted God's people since the beginning. While even the best of human beings err or stray, God never does. The mountains may fall, and the seas roar, "the nations rage, the kingdoms totter; he utters his voice, the earth melts" (Psalm 46:6). At a cancer bed, in the unemployment line, facing rejection from family or friends, the Christian can have rock-solid certainty that one thing will never change: God! "Jesus Christ is the same yesterday and today and forever" (Hebrews 13:8). The truth of God's faithfulness gives stability to the wavering, courage to the cowardly, conviction to the doubting, and eternal confidence to all who trust in Him. To be sure, the Bible also acknowledges that in this life it does not always *seem* as if God is being faithful. The Bible includes lament, most obviously in the book of Lamentations, over suffering and pain and disaster. Yet, even in suffering, the witness of the Bible and the testimony of God's people is that He is faithful. The most famous verse from the book of Lamentations is this: "The steadfast love of the LORD never ceases; his mercies never come to an end; they are new every morning; great is your faithfulness" (Lamentations 3:22-23). Or as Thomas Chisholm put it in the much beloved hymn, "Great is thy faithfulness! Great is thy faithfulness! Morning by morning new mercies I see; all I have needed thy hand hath provided: great is thy faithfulness, Lord, unto me!"

Psalm 36:5 NLT

Your unfailing love, O Lord,
is as vast as the heavens;
your faithfulness reaches beyond the clouds.

Psalm 86:15 NLT

But you, O Lord, are a God of compassion and mercy,
slow to get angry and filled with unfailing love and faithfulness.

Psalm 11[illegible]0 NASB

Your faithfulness continu[illegible]oughout generations;
You established the [illegible], and it stands.

Proverbs [illegible]0 NKJV

The name of the Lo[illegible] strong tower;
The righteous ru[illegible]and are safe.

1 Thessalonians 5:23-24 NLT

Now may the God of peace make you holy in every way,
and may your whole spirit and soul and body be kept blameless
until our Lord Jesus Christ comes again.
God will make this happen,
for he who calls you is faithful.

Hebrews 13:8 NASB

Jesus Christ is the same yesterday and today, and forever.

James 1:[illegible]IV

Every good gift and every pe[illegible]gift is from above,
coming down from the Fathe[illegible]e heavenly lights,
who does not change lik[illegible]ing shadows.

1 John 1:[illegible]KJV

If we confess our sins, He is faithfu[illegible]ust to forgive us our sins
and to cleanse us from a[illegible]ghteousness.

He shows mercy from
generation to generation
to all who fear him.
Luke 1:50 NLT

Knowi[illegible] God as Me[illegible]iful

Sometimes we get the impres[illegible]hat God is somehow less merciful than people, but the [illegible] reveals that the reverse is true. Yes, God's holiness is gre[illegible]han that of any person. As a result, His justice is greater [illegible]ours as well. Nonetheless, God shows over and over in H[illegible]lings with people that He is merciful. David witnesses to [illegible]hen he says to the prophet Gad that he would rather be di[illegible]hed by God than by people for God is merciful: "I am in g[illegible]istress. Let us fall into the hand of the LORD, for His merc[illegible]eat; but let me not fall into the hand of man" (2 Samuel 24[illegible]he mercies of God compel Nehemiah to rebuild Jerusale[illegible] great is our God, and also *how merciful*. Who would not [illegible]serve Him! (see Nehemiah 9:17, 31). Similarly, Psalm 23 m[illegible]s at the mercy of God. Ultimately, the Lord Jesus Himself [illegible]final and fullest expression of God's mercy (Luke 1:50). Pa[illegible]scribes the wonders of the gospel. At the end of a long doc[illegible] explanation in the book of Romans, he looks back and su[illegible]izes this good news as "the mercies of God." Such mercy [illegible]tes us to offer up our lives as living sacrifices (Romans 12[illegible]en Paul breaks into praise, it is the mercy of God that capt[illegible]is heart and mind: "Blessed be the God and Father of our [illegible]Jesus Christ, the Father of mercies and God of all comfor[illegible]orinthians 1:3).

Deuteronomy 4:31 NIV

For the Lord your God is a merciful God;
he will not abandon or destroy you
or forget the covenant with your ancestors,
which he confirmed to them by oath.

Nehemiah 9:17 NKJV

They refused to obey,
and they were not mindful
of Your wonders that You did among them.
But they hardened their necks,
and in their rebellion they appointed a leader
to return to their bondage.
But You are God, ready to pardon,
gracious and merciful, slow to anger,
abundant in kindness, and did not forsake them.

Psalm 2[illegible] KJV

Surely goodness and m[illegible]hall follow me
all the days [illegible]ife:
and I will dwell in the hou[illegible]he Lord forever.

Micah 7[illegible] NIV

Who is a God like you[illegible] pardons sin
and forgives the [illegible]ression
of the remnant of [illegible]eritance?
You do not stay [illegible] forever
but delight to s[illegible]ercy.

Romans 12:1 NIV

Therefore, I urge you, brothers and sisters,
in view of God's mercy,
to offer your bodies as a living sacrifice,
holy and pleasing to God—this is your true and proper worship.

2 Corinthians 1:3 NKJV

Blessed be the God and Father of our Lord Jesus Christ,
the Father of mercies and God of all comfort.

Ephesians 2:4-5 NLT

But God is so rich in mercy, and he loved us so much,
that even though we were dead because of our sins,
he gave us life when he raised Christ from the dead.
(It is only by God's grace that you have been saved!)

Hebrews 4:16 NKJV

Let us therefore come boldly to the throne of grace,
that we may obtain mercy and find grace to help in time of need.

Blessed is the one whose transgression is forgiven, whose sin is covered.
Psalm 32:1 ESV

Knowing God as Forgiving

A cynic might quip "Of course God will forgive me; that's His job!" But is it really so easy or simple? After all, God's "job" is also to be holy and to execute justice. Much of the Bible is concerned with the question, *How can a God of justice and holiness accept (let alone forgive) sinners like us?* The Old Testament solution centered around sacrifice. The extensive sacrificial codes of Leviticus are an expansion of the first "sacrifice" in the Garden when God used the skin of an animal to cover Adam and Eve's shame. The trouble with the sacrificial system was that it tended to become perfunctory (*Of course God will forgive...*). The prophets denounced such misuse of the sacrifices (Amos 5:21-22). This concern was reflected also in Jesus' quotation of Hosea 6:6 in Matthew 9:13, "Go and learn what this means, 'I desire mercy, and not sacrifice.' For I have come not to call the righteous, but sinners." Thoughtful Old Testament believers must have asked themselves how a mere lamb could take away a human's sins? God gave an answer in Christ—the lamb of God who takes away the sin of the world (John 1:29). Now, as *forgiven* people we must be *forgiving* people (Matthew 6:12) and preach the message that forgiveness comes through repentance and faith (Acts 2:38). When we grasp that truth, we are transformed by it. The message of forgiveness in Christ has the power to turn the world upside down!

Numbers 14:18 NLT

The Lord is slow to anger and filled with unfailing love,
forgiving every kind of sin and rebellion.
But he does not excuse the guilty.
He lays the sins of the parents upon their children;
the entire family is affected—
even children in the third and fourth generations.

2 Chronicles 7:14 NIV

If my people, who are called by my name,
will humble themselves and pray
and seek my face and turn from their wicked ways,
then I will hear from heaven,
and I will forgive their sin
and will heal their land.

Psalm 103:12 KJV

As far as the east is from the west,
so far hath he removed our transgressions from us.

Isaiah 1:18 KJV

Come now, and let us reason together, saith the Lord:
though your sins be as scarlet, they shall be as white as snow;
though they be red like crimson, they shall be as wool.

Matthew 6:12 NKJV

Forgive us our debts, as we forgive our debtors.

Acts 2:38 NIV

Peter replied, "Repent and be baptized, every one of you,
in the name of Jesus Christ for the forgiveness of your sins.
And you will receive the gift of the Holy Spirit."

Ephesians 4:32 NIV

Be kind and compassionate to one another, forgiving each other, just as in Christ God forgave you.

Colossians 1:13-14 NLT

For he has rescued us from the kingdom of darkness and transferred us into the Kingdom of his dear Son, who purchased our freedom and forgave our sins.

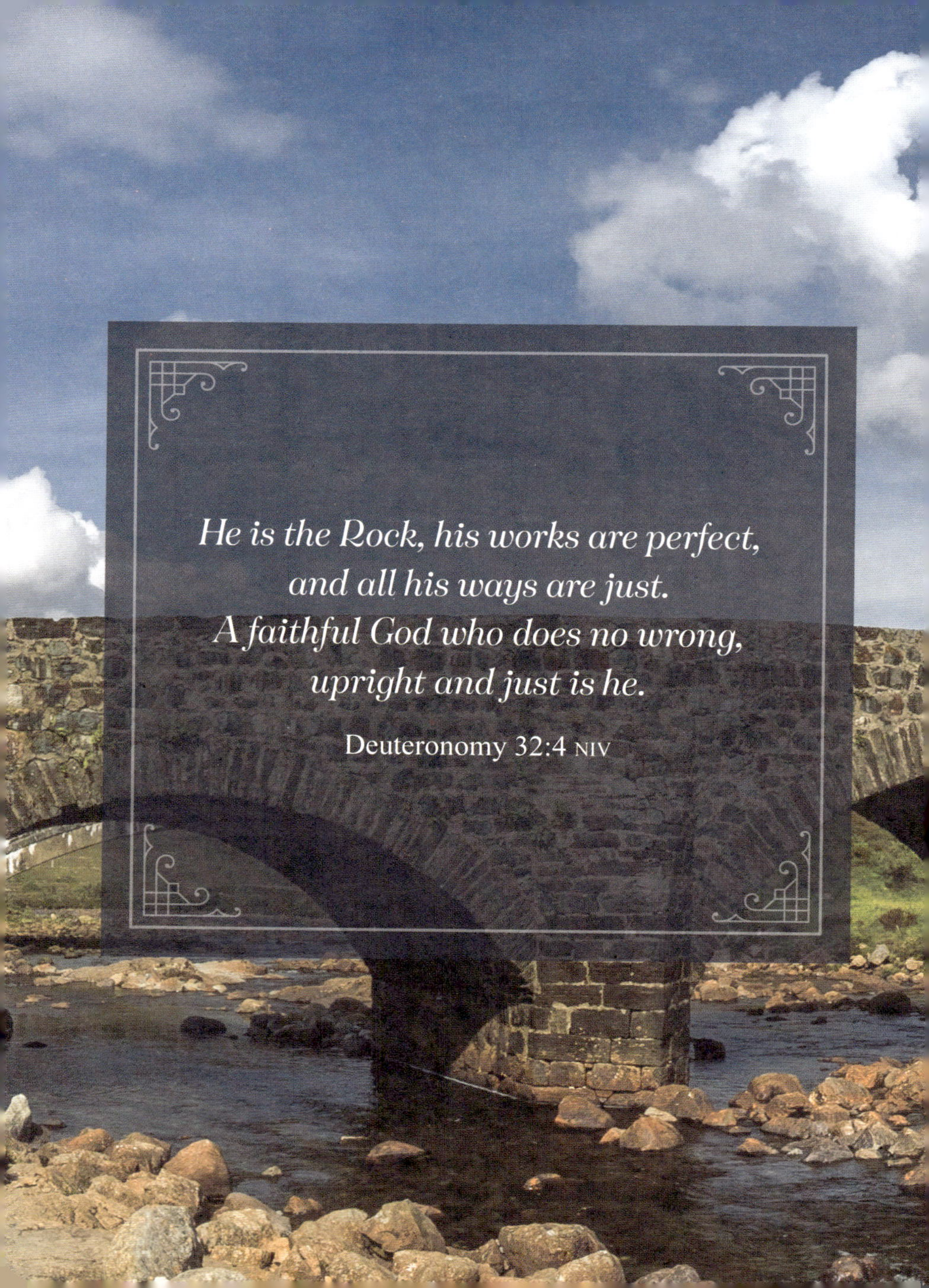
*He is the Rock, his works are perfect,
and all his ways are just.
A faithful God who does no wrong,
upright and just is he.*
Deuteronomy 32:4 NIV

Knowing God as Just

The justice of God is a core part of His character. It is not only who He is; it is how He behaves. Moses famously sings of God, "The Rock, His work is perfect, for all His ways are justice. A God of faithfulness and without iniquity, just and upright is He" (Deuteronomy 32:4). God's ways "are justice" because "just and upright is He." God acts in justice because He is just. The Psalmist picks up another theme regarding God being just—His justice is particularly concerned with the "oppressed" (Psalm 146:7). God does not play favorites. His justice is not good news for the privileged and bad news for those who cannot afford fancy lawyers. God is utterly fair, which means that, even for the oppressed, there is justice. Injustice will be punished, and things will be made right. But that day is not yet perfectly realized. We experience aspects of God's justice in the record of King David's good rule or in the good rule of some other human leader or judge. But oftentimes we long for justice—a state of "things-being-right" that is still to come. We cry out with Amos: "But let justice roll down like waters, and righteousness like an ever-flowing stream" (Amos 5:24). When Jesus speaks of justice, He makes it clear that outward religiosity is no cover for practical injustice. In fact, He takes the religious leaders of His day to task for their lack of justice despite their religious pomp. Jesus says to the leaders, "[You] have neglected the weightier matters of the law: justice and mercy and faithfulness ... You blind guides, straining out a gnat and swallowing a camel!" (Matthew 23:23-24). It is important to remember that none of us humans are really just (or righteous) by our own merits. It is by the gospel that we are made right, and in the power of the gospel that we then seek to do right. "For in [the gospel] the righteousness of God is revealed from faith for faith, as it is written, 'The righteous shall live by faith'" (Romans 1:17).

Psalm 37:27-29 NLT

Turn from evil and do good,
and you will live in the land forever.
For the LORD loves justice,
and he will never abandon the godly.
He will keep them safe forever,
but the children of the wicked will die.
The godly will possess the land
and will live there forever.

Psalm 140:12 NIV

I know that the LORD secures justice for the poor
and upholds the cause of the needy.

Psalm 146:7 NKJV

Who executes justice for the oppressed,
Who gives food to the hungry.
The LORD gives freedom to the prisoners.

Isaiah 30:18 NASB

Therefore the LORD longs to be gracious to you,
And therefore He waits on high to have compassion on you.
For the LORD is a God of justice;
How blessed are all those who long for Him.

Amos 5:24 ESV

But let justice roll down like waters,
and righteousness like an ever-flowing stream.

Matthew 23:23 NKJV

Woe to you, scribes and Pharisees, hypocrites!
For you pay tithe of mint and anise and cummin,
and have neglected the weightier matters of the law:
justice and mercy and faith.
These you ought to have done,
without leaving the others undone.

Romans 1:17 NIV

For in the gospel the righteousness of God is revealed—
a righteousness that is by faith from first to last,
just as it is written: "The righteous will live by faith."

Romans 3:23-26 NIV

For all have sinned and fall short of the glory of God,
and all are justified freely by his grace
through the redemption that came by Christ Jesus.
God presented Christ as a sacrifice of atonement,
through the shedding of his blood—to be received by faith.
He did this to demonstrate his righteousness,
because in his forbearance
he had left the sins committed beforehand unpunished—
he did it to demonstrate his righteousness at the present time,
so as to be just and the one who justifies
those who have faith in Jesus

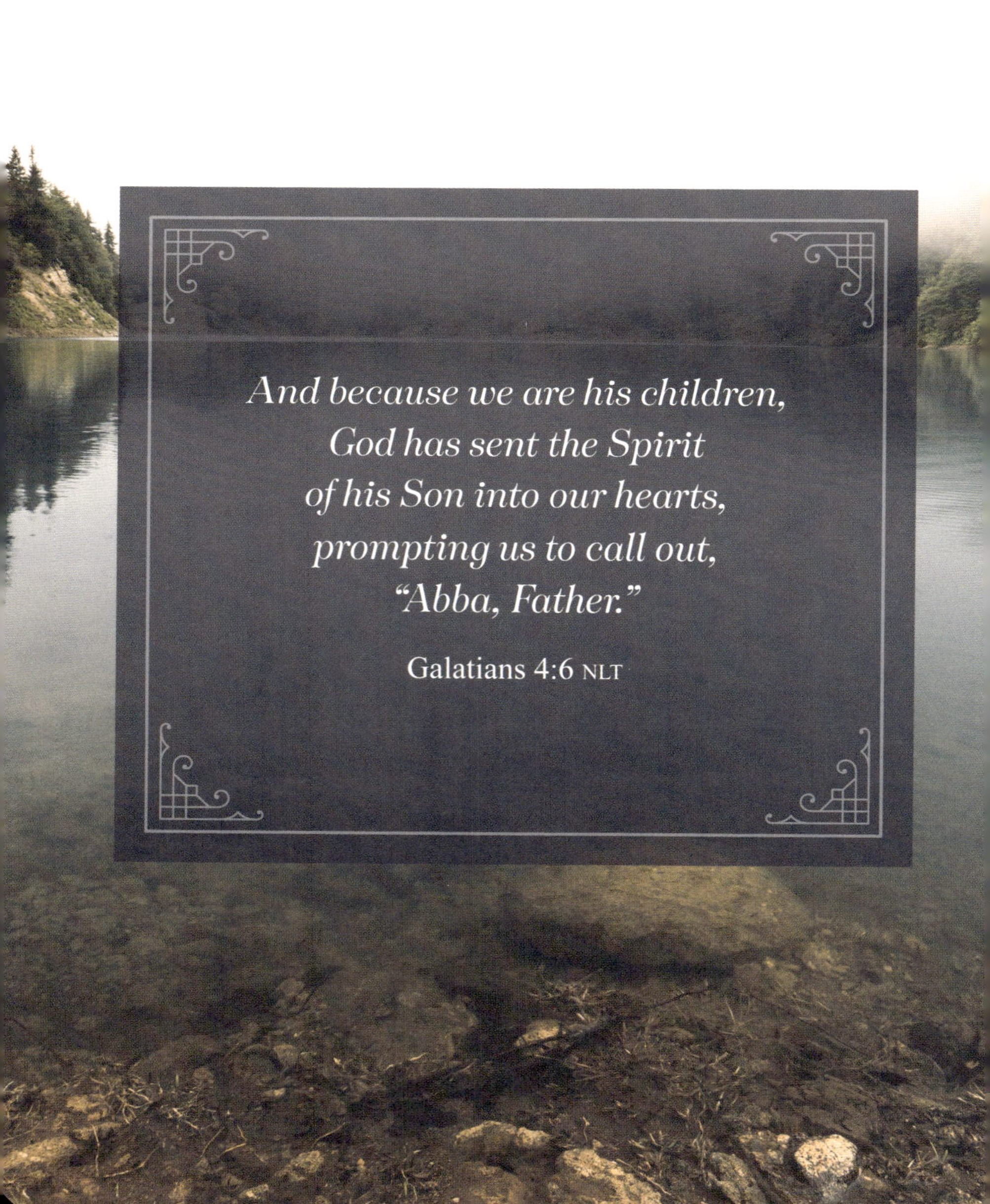

And because we are his children,
God has sent the Spirit
of his Son into our hearts,
prompting us to call out,
"Abba, Father."

Galatians 4:6 NLT

Knowing God as Father

The Old Testament does not often describe God as "Father." The most obvious reference is in Isaiah 64:8, "But now, O Lord, you are our Father; we are the clay, and you are our potter; we are all the work of your hand." The idea of God as Father is seen in references to God's people being God's "son." For instance, in Exodus 4:22 God says, "Israel is my firstborn son." Deuteronomy 32:6 refers to God as "Father" and "Creator." Famously, Psalm 103:13 says, "As a father shows compassion to his children, so the Lord shows compassion to those who fear him." There is no doubt, though, that Jesus emphasized the idea of God as Father and encouraged His disciples to call God *Father*. Knowing God as Father is the key, in many ways, to the famous Lord's Prayer which begins, "Our Father in heaven, hallowed be your name" (Matthew 6:9). Thereafter, the New Testament writers follow Jesus' teaching and attribute to God the name *Father* in many places: Romans 1:17, 1 Corinthians 8:6, Galatians 1:3. Why the change from the Old Testament to the New? Because Jesus made God known in a new and fuller way: "No one has ever seen God; the only God, who is at the Father's side, He has made him known" (John 1:18). Jesus made it clear that we, through faith, may approach the living God as our Father too. Jesus said, "I am ascending to My Father and your Father, to My God and your God" (John 20:17 NLT). Amazingly, we may now, by faith in Jesus, in the intimacy and power of the Spirit, call God our "Abba, Father" (Mark 14:36; Galatians 4:6).

Psalm 103:13 ESV

As a father shows compassion to his children,
so the LORD shows compassion to those who fear him.

Isaiah 64:8 NKJV

But now, O LORD,
You are our Father;
We are the clay, and You our potter;
And all we are the work of Your hand.

Hosea 11:1-3 NLT

"When Israel was a child, I loved him,
and I called my son out of Egypt.
But the more I called to him, the farther he moved from me,
offering sacrifices to the images of Baal and burning incense to idols.
I myself taught Israel how to walk, leading him along by the hand.
But he doesn't know or even care that it was I who took care of him."

Matthew 12:50 NASB

For whoever does the will of My Father who is in heaven,
he is My brother, and sister, and mother.

Mark 14:36 NKJV

And He said, "Abba, Father, all things are possible for You.
Take this cup away from Me;
nevertheless, not what I will, but what You will."

John 1:18 NIV

No one has ever seen God; but the one and only Son,
who is himself God and is in closest relationship with the Father,
has made him known.

1 Corinthians 8:6 NLT

There is one God, the Father,
by whom all things were created,
and for whom we live.
And there is one Lord, Jesus Christ,
through whom all things were created,
and through whom we live.

Romans 8:16 ESV

The Spirit himself bears witness with our spirit
that we are children of God.

And the Word became
flesh and dwelt among us,
and we have seen his glory,
glory as of the only
Son from the Father,
full of grace and truth.
John 1:14 ESV

Knowing God as Son

We typically think of the Sonship of God—the doctrine that Jesus is the Son of God—as being a distinctly New Testament teaching. But there are glimpses of this idea in the Old Testament too. When Joshua meets the captain of the Lord's army in Joshua 5:13-15, he encounters the kind of holiness that is only true of God. At the same time, the captain also seems to have human form. Many think this is an example of Jesus appearing before He was born to Mary. In addition to such pre-incarnate appearances of the Son of God in the Old Testament (see Daniel 3:24-25), the New Testament helps us to see that Jesus is the king spoken of in Psalm 2 and the child named Immanuel in Isaiah 7. Of course, the reality that the "Son of God" is Jesus is only explained fully in the New Testament. The first chapter of John majestically declares that the Word became flesh, and we have seen His glory—the glory of the one and only Son. Philippians 2 wonders at the humility of the Son who became human to bear the punishment that we deserved. Paul calls everyone to bow before this Jesus. Colossians 1 tells us that Jesus is the very image of the invisible God. If we asked the question, *What is God like?* The answer of the New Testament (at least in a very simplified form) would be, *God is like Jesus because Jesus, God's Son, is also fully and completely God.* (We will learn more about the nature of the Trinity, but a good explanation can be found in the historic Athanasian Creed.) Still, how amazing it is, that if we had been born at the right time, and in the right place, if we had wandered around Galilee, we would have met God incarnate!

Psalm 2:7 ESV

I will tell of the decree:
The LORD said to me, "You are my Son;
today I have begotten you."

Isaiah 7:14 KJV

Therefore the LORD himself shall give you a sign;
Behold, a virgin shall conceive, and bear a son,
and shall call his name Immanuel.

Matthew 3:17 NIV

And a voice from heaven said,
"This is my Son, whom I love; with him I am well pleased."

Matthew 11:27 NASB

All things have been handed over to Me by My Father;
and no one knows the Son except the Father;
nor does anyone know the Father except the Son,
and anyone to whom the Son determines to reveal Him.

John 20:31 NIV

But these are written that you may believe
that Jesus is the Messiah, the Son of God,
and that by believing you may have life in his name.

Philippians 2:10 NKJV

At the name of Jesus every knee should bow,
of those in heaven, and of those on earth,
and of those under the earth.

Colossians 1:15 NLT

Christ is the visible image of the invisible God.
He existed before anything was created
and is supreme over all creation.

Hebrews 1:3 NIV

The Son is the radiance of God's glory
and the exact representation of his being,
sustaining all things by his powerful word.
After he had provided purification for sins,
he sat down at the right hand of the Majesty in heaven.

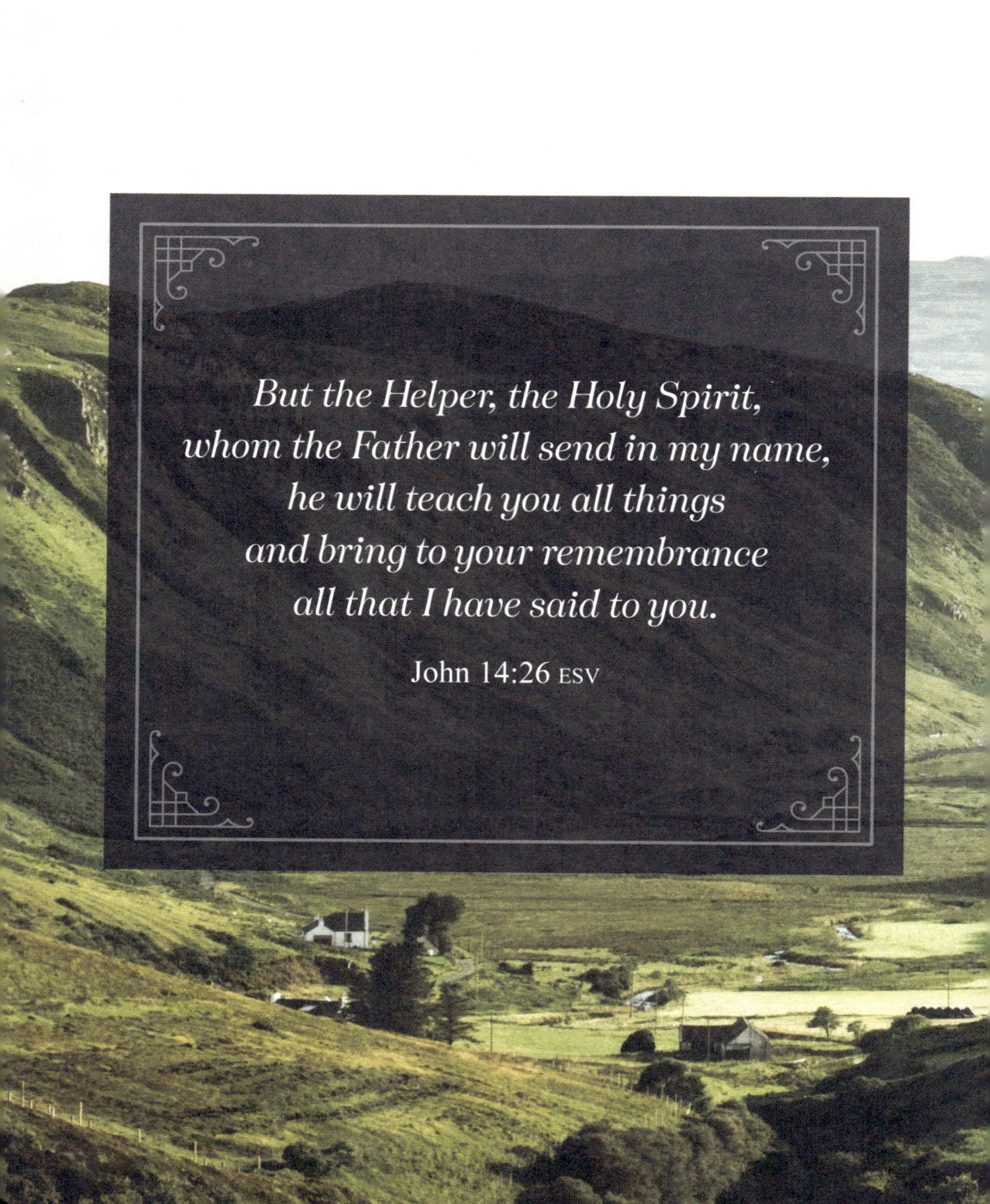
But the Helper, the Holy Spirit,
whom the Father will send in my name,
he will teach you all things
and bring to your remembrance
all that I have said to you.
John 14:26 ESV

Knowing God as Holy Spirit

Many people find that the Holy Spirit is the hardest member of the Trinity to understand. This should be no surprise: He (yes, Jesus calls the Spirit *He*, not *it*) is after all Spirit, and spiritual things are more difficult for us to comprehend. Jesus' analogy to explain the Spirit is both deep and simple: "The wind blows where it wishes, and you hear its sound, but you do not know where it comes from or where it is goes. So it is with everyone born of the Spirit" (John 3:8). The Spirit appears in the very first verse of the Bible (Genesis 1:1), and the Spirit is coeternal with God the Father and God the Son (which means He also has no beginning or ending). Although the Spirit is present and active in the Old Testament, there is a special and new work of the Spirit that comes with the New Testament, and with Pentecost in particular. Jesus promises us the Spirit, a promise so great that Jesus even suggested it would be better for Him to leave so that His followers could receive the Spirit (John 16:7). The Spirit gifts God's people for works of service (1 Corinthians 12-14; Ephesians 4), and He enables us to pursue increasing Christlikeness as we "walk in the Spirit" (Galatians 5:16-26). Amazingly, the Spirit "intercedes" for us with "groanings too deep for words" (Romans 8:26) which provides great comfort for us in our trials. At Pentecost, the Spirit came with fresh power to enable God's people to take the gospel to all nations (Acts 2). Ephesians 1:13 says that upon trusting Jesus as our Lord, the Spirit is given to us as the "seal" of our salvation. However, the degree to which we experience the power and presence of the Spirit can ebb and flow and must be refreshed by God's Word, worship, prayer, and fellowship with other believers (Ephesians 5:18). Finally, the Bible teaches that we are in a battle, and we fight that battle with the sword of the Spirit which is the Word of God (Ephesians 6:17).

Genesis 1:2 KJV

And the earth was without form, and void;
and darkness was upon the face of the deep.
And the Spirit of God moved upon the face of the waters.

Ezekiel 36:27 NLT

And I will put my Spirit in you
so that you will follow my decrees
and be careful to obey my regulations.

Joel 2:28-29 NIV

And afterward, I will pour out my Spirit on all people.
Your sons and daughters will prophesy,
your old men will dream dreams,
your young men will see visions.
Even on my servants, both men and women,
I will pour out my Spirit in those days.

John 3:8 ESV

The wind blows where it wishes, and you hear its sound,
but you do not know where it
comes from or where it goes.
So it is with everyone who is born of the Spirit.

John 16:13 NASB

But when He, the Spirit of truth, comes,
He will guide you into all the truth;
for He will not speak on His own,
but whatever He hears, He will speak;
and He will disclose to you what is to come.

Romans 5:5 NKJV

Now hope does not disappoint,
because the love of God has been poured out in our hearts
by the Holy Spirit who was given to us.

Romans 8:26 NIV

In the same way, the Spirit helps us in our weakness.
We do not know what we ought to pray for,
but the Spirit himself intercedes for us through wordless groans.

Ephesians 1:13-14 NIV

And you also were included in Christ
when you heard the message of truth,
the gospel of your salvation.
When you believed, you were marked in him with a seal,
the promised Holy Spirit,
who is a deposit guaranteeing our inheritance
until the redemption of those
who are God's possession—to the praise of his glory.

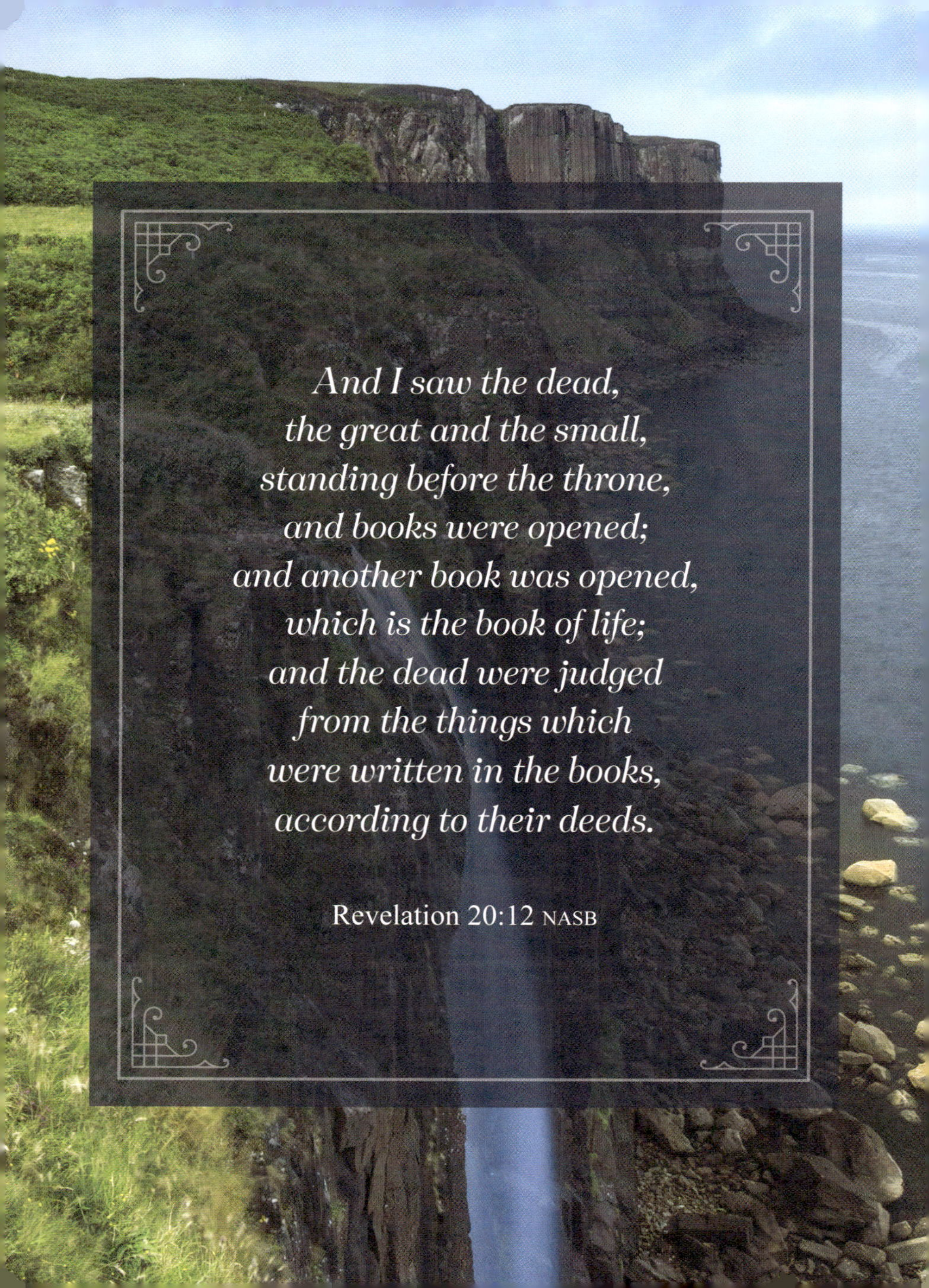
And I saw the dead,
the great and the small,
standing before the throne,
and books were opened;
and another book was opened,
which is the book of life;
and the dead were judged
from the things which
were written in the books,
according to their deeds.
Revelation 20:12 NASB

Knowing God as Judge

There are few more fearful doctrines than the doctrine of judgment (except perhaps the doctrine of eternal punishment which follows from judgment). Who can think of such things without trembling? It is a fearful thing to fall into the hands of the living God. Ever since humans rebelled, our world has existed under a sentence of death and hell. All the deeds of this world, secret as well as overt, will one day be judged by God who judges righteously. What hope is there for any of us? Only that Christ, who was perfectly righteous, was judged for us, and now "there is therefore no condemnation for those who are in Christ Jesus" (Romans 8:1). Jesus Himself teaches us the same—that whoever believes in Him is "not condemned" (John 3:18). We will not be condemned, but even Christians will give an answer for how they have spent the life that their Lord has given to them and whether they have built on the foundation with precious gold or with hay (1 Corinthians 3:13). So "the judgment day" stands as a dire warning to any who are outside of Christ *and* as a motivation to bear fruit for God's glory for those who are in Christ. The famous passage in Matthew 25:31-46 about the separation of the sheep from the goats appears at first glance to depend entirely upon our active practical works. A closer reading shows us that the kingdom given to the "sheep"—those who are righteous—is an "inherited" kingdom "prepared" for them. It is not based upon their merits. Instead, their godly deeds of charity bear witness to the reality that they belong to the kingdom and have inherited what was prepared for them. Faith is seen by our works. James teaches that faith without works is no real faith (James 2:22), and Paul agrees that faith must express itself in love (Galatians 5:6). With this teaching about judgment in mind, let us come to Christ to save us and, as saved people, be inspired to live fruitful lives for His glory.

Genesis 3:24 NASB

So He drove the man out; and at the east of the Garden of Eden
He stationed the cherubim and the flaming sword
which turned every direction to guard the way to the tree of life.

Matthew 25:32 NASB

And all the nations will be gathered before Him;
and He will separate them from one another,
just as the shepherd separates the sheep from the goats.

John 3:18 NKJV

He who believes in Him is not condemned;
but he who does not believe is condemned already,
because he has not believed
in the name of the only begotten Son of God.

Romans 6:23 NASB

For the wages of sin is death,
but the gracious gift of God is eternal life
in Christ Jesus our Lord.

Romans 8:1 NIV

Therefore, there is now no condemnation
for those who are in Christ Jesus.

1 Corinthians 4:5 NLT

So don't make judgments about anyone ahead of time—
before the Lord returns.
For he will bring our darkest secrets
to light and will reveal our private motives.
Then God will give to each one whatever praise is due.

2 Corinthians 5:10 NKJV

For we must all appear before the judgment seat of Christ,
that each one may receive the things done in the body,
according to what he has done, whether good or bad.

2 Peter 2:9 NLT

So you see, the Lord knows how to rescue
godly people from their trials,
even while keeping the wicked
under punishment until the day of final judgment.

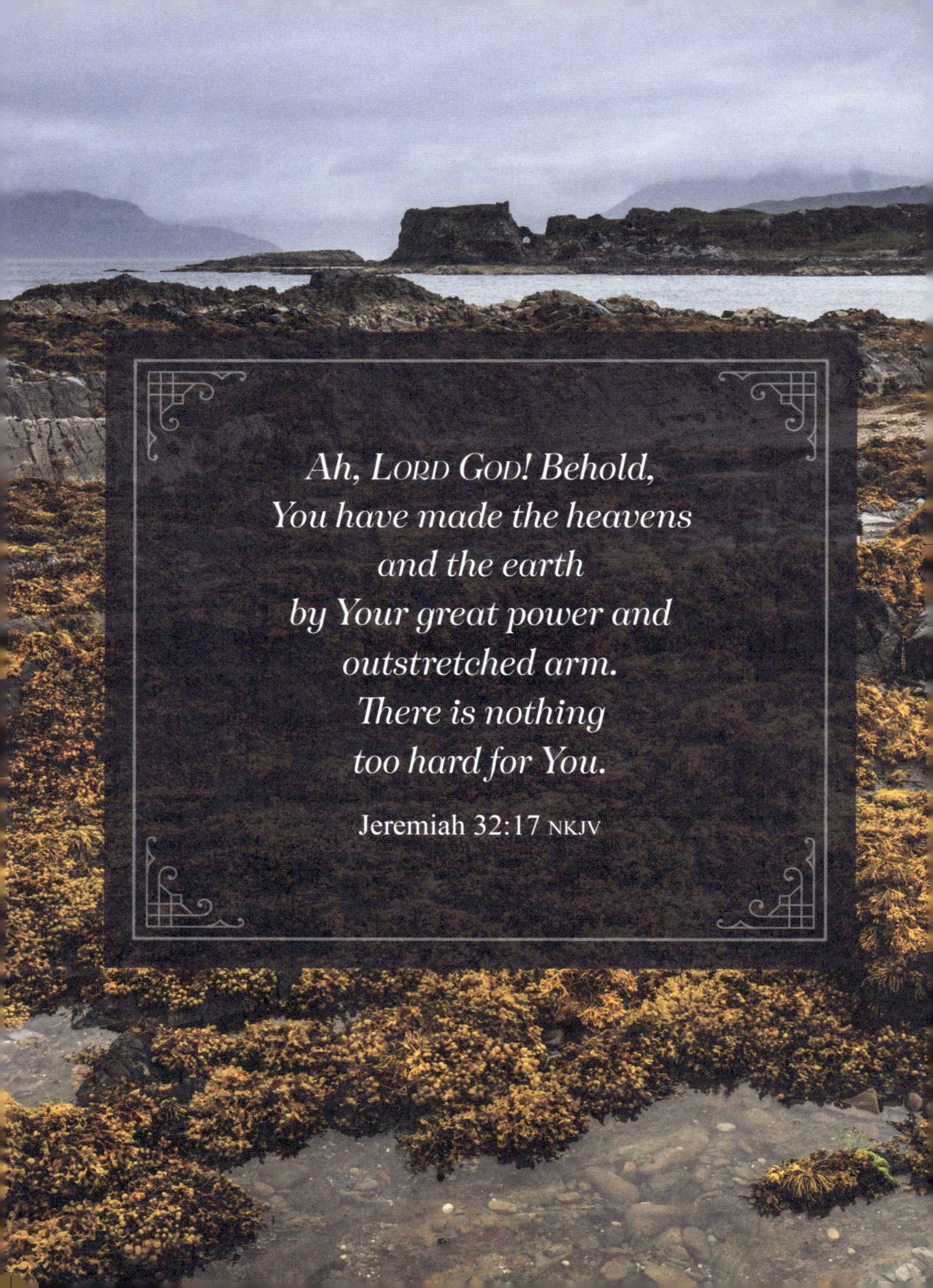
Ah, Lord God! Behold,
You have made the heavens
and the earth
by Your great power and
outstretched arm.
There is nothing
too hard for You.
Jeremiah 32:17 NKJV

Knowing God as All-Powerful

Part of the biblical definition of God is that He is omnipotent or all-powerful. To have power over all things is what it means to be God. We see God's omnipotence played out in various significant ways throughout the Bible but particularly in creation. God speaks, and it is done. Divine power is on display from the very beginning. We also see evidence of God's power in that that He knows everything we think and do, and He even shapes our thinking as well as our doing (Psalm 139, Proverbs 21:1). The power of God is certainly not God's only attribute. Of course, He is also loving and holy. God is not an evil dictator. But He is God—immeasurably and inconceivably powerful. What is more, God's power is displayed not only in creation but also in salvation. The apostle Paul tells the story of God's power to save in his amazing introduction to the letter of Ephesians and in Romans 9–11. But Jesus Himself confirms the power upholding our salvation: "I give them eternal life, and they will never perish, and no one can snatch them out of my hand" (John 10:28). Faith rests in God's promise to save and His power enabling Him to keep that promise despite any threat. The truth that God is powerful to keep His promises is what Sarah should have understood (Genesis 18:14) and what Mary commendably did understand (Luke 1:37). I expect belief in the power of God is the key to Christian bravery, and at least Paul appears to agree with me when he urges the Ephesians to "be strong in the Lord and in the strength of his might" (Ephesians 6:10). Meditate on God's power to accomplish all of His purposes: *He has promised, He can, and He will.*

Genesis 18:14 NASB

Is anything too difficult for the Lord?
At the appointed time I will return to you,
at this time next year, and Sarah will have a son.

1 Chronicles 29:11 NLT

Yours, O Lord, is the greatness, the power,
the glory, the victory, and the majesty.
Everything in the heavens and on earth is yours,
O Lord, and this is your kingdom.
We adore you as the one who is over all things.

Psalm 147:4-5 NIV

He determines the number of the stars and
calls them each by name.
Great is our Lord and mighty in power;
his understanding has no limit.

Isaiah 41:10 NKJV

Fear not, for I am with you; Be not dismayed, for I am your God.
I will strengthen you, Yes, I will help you,
I will uphold you with My righteous right hand.

Mark 10:27 NASB

Looking at them, Jesus said,
"With people it is impossible, but not with God;
for all things are possible with God."

Luke 1:37 NASB

For nothing will be impossible with God.

Romans 1:20 NIV

For since the creation of the world God's invisible qualities—
his eternal power and divine nature—have been clearly seen,
being understood from what has been made,
so that people are without excuse.

Ephesians 1:11 NLT

Furthermore, because we are united with Christ,
we have received an inheritance from God,
for he chose us in advance,
and he makes everything work out according to his plan.

Great is our Lord,
and of great power:
his understanding is infinite.
Psalm 147:5 KJV

Knowing God as All-Knowing

The biblical teaching that God is omniscient or "all-knowing" is clear and irrefutable. But we sometimes confuse two aspects of God's knowledge which overlap, even though they are distinct. The Bible does teach that God knows everything in the sense that we normally attribute such knowledge to God. He has infinite knowledge. Nothing is hidden from Him. He knows the stars and the molecules and the subatomic particles. He even knows our hidden thoughts. But the Bible also teaches that God knows His people in the sense that He has a personal relationship with them. So when Paul tells us that God "foreknew" us (Romans 8:29), he is not merely teaching that God knew us beforehand in an intellectual sense of cognition or awareness. He is teaching us that God loves us and knows us relationally. That theme of God's personal, intimate, knowledge of us is reflected in the prophecy of Hosea. "I know Ephraim, and Israel is not hidden from me" (Hosea 5:3); or earlier, "I will betroth you to me in faithfulness. And you shall know the LORD" (Hosea 2:20). In Hosea, the covenant knowledge of husband and wife is used to describe the knowledge that God has of His people. When we think of God's knowledge, we are also to think of His love and His relationship to us. This loving relationship and deep understanding are also part of God's infinite knowledge.

Psalm 139:1-6 NASB

LORD, You have searched me and known me.
You know when I sit down and when I get up;
You understand my thought from far away.
You scrutinize my path and my lying down,
And are acquainted with all my ways.
Even before there is a word on my tongue,
Behold, LORD, You know it all.
You have encircled me behind and in front,
And placed Your hand upon me.
Such knowledge is too wonderful for me;
It is too high, I cannot comprehend it.

Proverbs 15:3 NKJV

The eyes of the LORD are in every place,
Keeping watch on the evil and the good.

Isaiah 55:8-9 NIV

"For my thoughts are not your thoughts,
neither are your ways my ways," declares the LORD.
"As the heavens are higher than the earth,
so are my ways higher than your ways
and my thoughts than your thoughts."

Hosea 2:19-20 NIV

I will betroth you to me forever;
I will betroth you in righteousness and justice,
in love and compassion.
I will betroth you in faithfulness,
and you will acknowledge the LORD.

Matthew 10:29-31 NIV

Are not two sparrows sold for a penny?
Yet not one of them will fall to the ground outside your Father's care.
And even the very hairs of your head are all numbered.
So don't be afraid; you are worth more than many sparrows.

Romans 11:33-36 NLT

Oh, how great are God's riches and wisdom and knowledge!
How impossible it is for us to understand his decisions and his ways!
For who can know the Lord's thoughts?
Who knows enough to give him advice?
And who has given him so much that he needs to pay it back?
For everything comes from him and exists by his power and is intended for his glory.
All glory to him forever! Amen.

Romans 8:29 NKJV

For whom He foreknew, He also predestined
to be conformed to the image of His Son,
that He might be the firstborn among many brethren.

1 John 3:20 KJV

For if our heart condemns us,
God is greater than our heart, and knows all things.

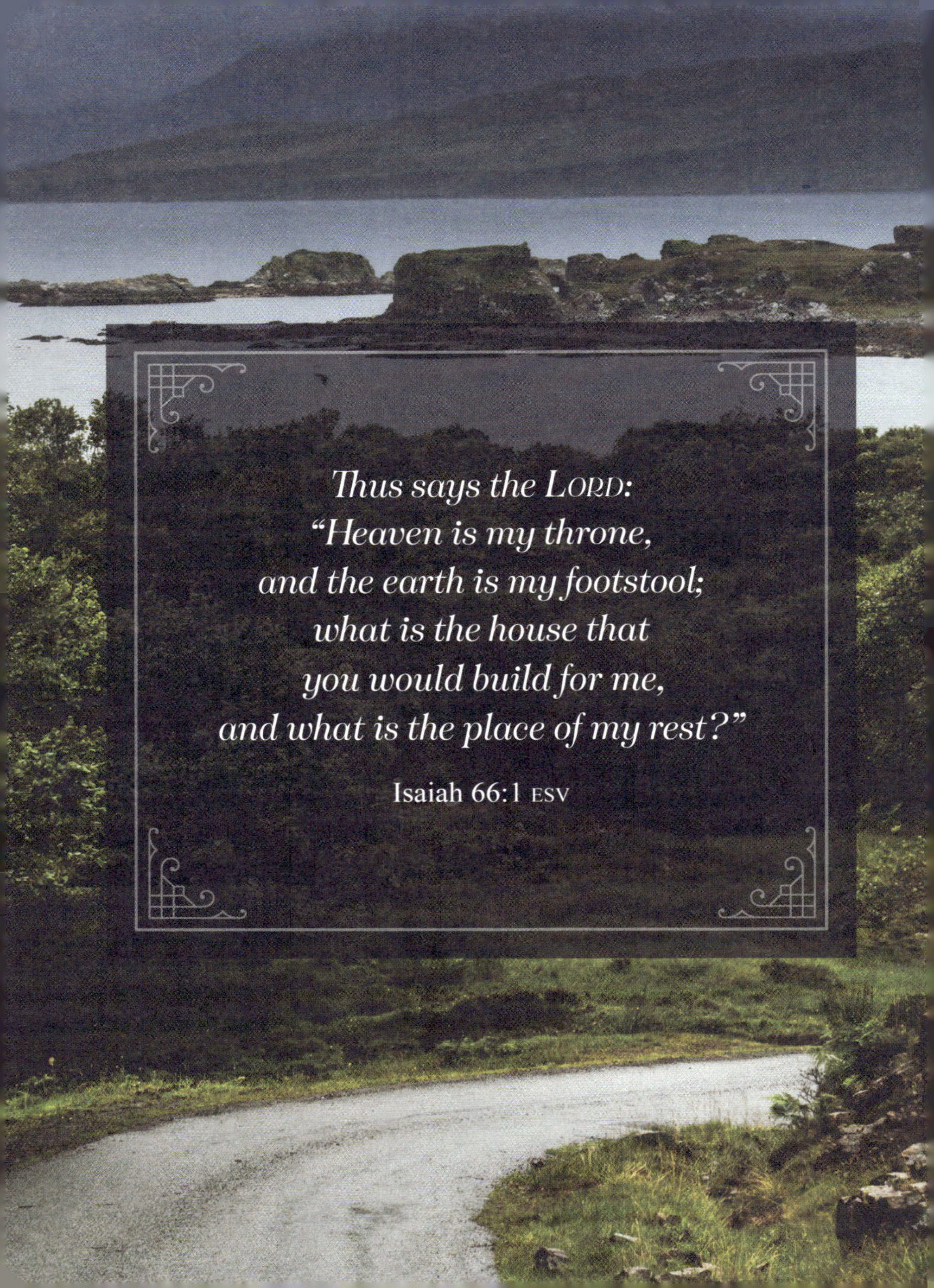
Thus says the Lord:
"Heaven is my throne,
and the earth is my footstool;
what is the house that
you would build for me,
and what is the place of my rest?"
Isaiah 66:1 ESV

Knowing God as Always Present

God's omnipresence (or that he is "always present") is another of His "incommunicable attributes." There are parts of who God is that we, made in His image, may share. For example, He is love, and we may love. But other characteristics of God are "incommunicable," that is they may not be shared by mere humans like us. His omnipotence (or being "all-powerful") is one of those incommunicable attributes, as is His omnipresence (being "always present"). Because God's omnipresence is incommunicable, it is hard for us to grasp exactly what it can mean. In what sense is God everywhere all the time? An illustration that some find helpful is to imagine what it would be like for a two-dimensional being to encounter a three-dimensional being. If you only exist in two-dimensions, you are only aware of length and breadth. A being that has a third dimension (height) would be able to see across the length and breadth of the two dimensions all the time and be even more involved in those two dimensions at certain moments. Now imagine that that there is (as there truly is) a fourth dimension—a spiritual reality around us. God would be able to be fully present all the time, while acting more powerfully at certain moments and times too. This is far from a perfect illustration (there are other spiritual beings which are *not* omnipresent: angels, for instance), but it might help you grasp something of the biblical teaching. "Thus says the Lord, 'Heaven is my throne and the earth is my footstool; what is the house that you would build for me, and what is the place of my rest?'" (Isaiah 66:1).

Deuteronomy 4:39 ESV

Know therefore today, and lay it to your heart,
that the Lord is God in heaven above
and on the earth beneath; there is no other.

Deuteronomy 31:6 NIV

Be strong and courageous.
Do not be afraid or terrified because of them,
for the Lord your God goes with you;
he will never leave you nor forsake you.

Psalm 139:7-10 NASB

Where can I go from Your Spirit?
Or where can I flee from Your presence?
If I ascend to heaven, You are there;
If I make my bed in Sheol, behold, You are there.
If I take up the wings of the dawn,
If I dwell in the remotest part of the sea,
Even there Your hand will lead me,
And Your right hand will take hold of me.

Isaiah 43:2 NASB

When you pass through the waters, I will be with you;
And through the rivers, they will not overflow you.
When you walk through the fire, you will not be scorched,
Nor will the flame burn you.

Jeremiah 23:24 KJV

Can any hide himself in secret places that I shall not see him? saith the LORD. Do not I fill heaven and earth? saith the LORD.

Acts 17:27 NLT

His purpose was for the nations to seek after God and perhaps feel their way toward him and find him—though he is not far from any one of us.

Ephesians 4:5-6 NLT

There is one Lord, one faith, one baptism,
one God and Father of all, who is over all,
in all, and living through all.

Revelation 21:3 ESV

And I heard a loud voice from the throne saying,
"Behold, the dwelling place of God is with man.
He will dwell with them, and they will be his people,
and God himself will be with them as their God."

Following God

*Those whom I love
I rebuke and discipline.
So be earnest and repent.*
Revelation 3:19 NIV

Following God with Repentance

It is one of the great errors of church history that the word for *repentance* was translated to mean "do penance" in the Vulgate (a Latin translation of the Bible that was used for more than a thousand years.) This mistranslation has led to unending confusion as to what the Bible means by repentance. The Greek word essentially means to "change your mind." The point of repentance is not that we must perform certain humiliating religious exercises to get ourselves back in God's favor. No, repentance simply stops running away from God and turns around to run toward Him. Biblically, the idea of repentance is rooted in the Old Testament promise that if God's people turned back to Him even after they had been idolatrous, God would forgive their sin and restore them to their homeland even after they were exiled to Assyria and Babylon. However, an even greater return from exile will come with the reign of King Jesus when we find ourselves at home in His kingdom. We must turn away from rejecting Jesus and turn back to accepting Jesus. If we do, our sins will be forgiven. Once we are Christians—people who trust Jesus and submit to Him as our King—we need to keep short accounts with God, to quickly say "sorry" and mean it when we sin. God will at times discipline us when we sin, but remember, discipline is His kindness to lead us back into vital and thrilling relationship with Him once again.

Psalm 51:17 NLT

The sacrifice you desire is a broken spirit.
You will not reject a broken and repentant heart, O God.

Proverbs 28:13 NASB

One who conceals his wrongdoings will not prosper,
But one who confesses and abandons them will find compassion.

Isaiah 30:15 NIV

This is what the Sovereign LORD, the Holy One of Israel, says:
"In repentance and rest is your salvation,
in quietness and trust is your strength,
but you would have none of it."

Joel 2:13 NKJV

So rend your heart, and not your garments;
Return to the LORD your God, For He is gracious and merciful,
Slow to anger, and of great kindness;
And He relents from doing harm.

Matthew 4:17 KJV

From that time Jesus began to preach, and to say,
Repent: for the kingdom of heaven is at hand.

Romans 2:4 NLT

Don't you see how wonderfully kind, tolerant,
and patient God is with you?
Does this mean nothing to you?
Can't you see that his kindness is intended
to turn you from your sin?

2 Corinthians 7:10 NKJV

For godly sorrow produces repentance leading to salvation, not to be regretted; but the sorrow of the world produces death.

2 Peter 3:9 ESV

The Lord is not slow to fulfill his promise as some count slowness, but is patient toward you, not wishing that any should perish, but that all should reach repentance.

Therefore being justified by faith,
we have peace with God
through our Lord Jesus Christ.
Romans 5:1 KJV

Following God with Faith

We use the word and concept of faith in at least three different, distinct, but interrelated ways. First, the word *faith* is used subjectively of individuals believing. (For instance, we will say someone trusts God or has personal faith in God.) Second, the word *faith* is used objectively to describe what is believed. (For instance, we will talk about "the faith" or "the Christian faith," meaning the doctrine or content of what is believed.) Third, the word *faith* is used of faithfulness or reliability, primarily of God but also of those who follow God and are faithful too. (For instance, we will say that someone "kept the faith" or was faithful, or we will say that God is faithful.) The apostle Paul teaches us that we are justified, or declared right before God, *by faith*—by trusting God personally and believing that He is faithful to keep His promises. Having been declared right before God, we are then gradually transformed to be more like God through our active participation in the process of becoming holy. The Spirit guides and helps us along the way. In other words, we are (as the Puritans put it) "justified by faith alone but not by faith that remains alone." Real faith transforms us—but it is always faith first, then works. Those who follow God are described as people of faith because they faithfully rely on God's promises through the ups and downs of life, not because they are perfect. The great roll call of faith in Hebrews 11 describes this kind of faith or faithfulness. Many of the heroes of faith in Hebrews 11 were at times less than perfect in how they lived, but they believed God and trusted Him. Let us follow the example of those heroes of faith and embrace the apostle Paul's teaching about trusting in God. Let us be people who also walk by faith for God's glory!

Psalm 119:30 ESV

I have chosen the way of faithfulness;
I set your rules before me.

Habakkuk 2:4 NKJV

Behold the proud,
His soul is not upright in him;
But the just shall live by his faith.

Romans 10:17 ESV

So faith comes from hearing,
and hearing through the word of Christ.

1 Corinthians 16:13-14 NIV

Be on your guard; stand firm in the faith;
be courageous; be strong.
Do everything in love.

2 Corinthians 5:7 KJV

For we walk by faith, not by sight.

Galatians 2:20 NIV

I have been crucified with Christ and I no longer live,
but Christ lives in me.
The life I now live in the body, I live by faith in the Son of God,
who loved me and gave himself for me.

Ephesians 2:8-9 NKJV

For by grace you have been saved through faith,
and that not of yourselves;
it is the gift of God, not of works, lest anyone should boast.

Hebrews 11:1-3 ESV

Now faith is the assurance of things hoped for,
the conviction of things not seen.
For by it the people of old received their commendation.
By faith we understand that the universe
was created by the word of God,
so that what is seen was not made out of things that are visible.

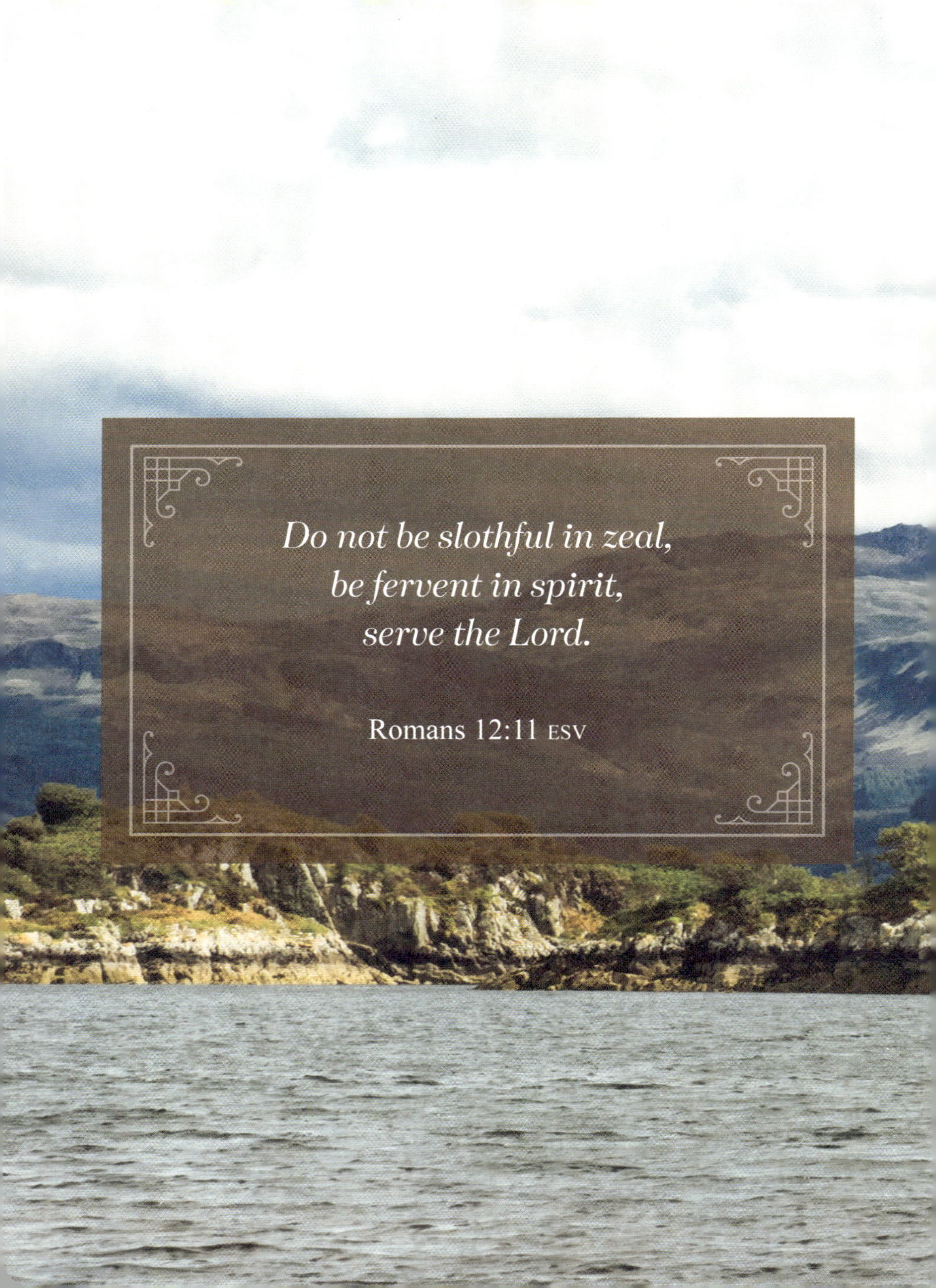
*Do not be slothful in zeal,
be fervent in spirit,
serve the Lord.*
Romans 12:11 ESV

Following God with Passion

The word "passion" itself technically refers to suffering (for instance, the "passion of the Christ" means Jesus' death on the cross), but we also use it to mean *zeal* or *fervor*. The Bible tells us that such passion or fervor even characterizes the concern that God has to save us! Isaiah prophesied that the Messiah would come and advance God's saving kingdom. It is the "zeal of the Lord of hosts [that] will do this" (Isaiah 9:7). In the life of Jesus, we see such zeal, particularly for people to worship God in truth and Spirit. The corruption of the temple at the time prevented such worship, so Jesus forcibly cleansed the temple. Jesus' disciples remembered this as a fulfilment of Psalm 69: "Zeal for your house will consume me" (John 2:17 NASB). Given that passion is characteristic of God, and therefore characteristic of the Lord Jesus, zeal is also to be characteristic of the followers of Jesus. But there is a caution which Paul addresses in Romans chapter 10. It is possible to have a kind of zeal for God that is "not according to knowledge" (Romans 10:2). In particular, Paul has in mind his own people who were zealous for God but had misunderstood the righteousness of God and were attempting to set up their own righteousness instead. While there can certainly be a misguided zeal, we must not think that *all* zeal is misguided! Indeed, Paul later says, "Do not be slothful in zeal, be fervent in spirit, serve the Lord" (Romans 12:11). This Christian zeal or passion or earnestness is to be rooted and grounded and expressed in love for God and for one another. As Peter puts it, "Above all, keep loving one another earnestly, since loves cover a multitude of sins" (1 Peter 4:8).

Isaiah 9:7 NKJV

Of the increase of His government and peace
There will be no end,
Upon the throne of David and over His kingdom,
To order it and establish it with judgment and justice
From that time forward, even forever.
The zeal of the LORD of hosts will perform this.

John 2:17 NASB

His disciples remembered that it was written:
"Zeal for Your house will consume me."

Romans 10:2 ESV

For I bear them witness that they have a zeal for God,
but not according to knowledge.

Philippians 1:27 NLT

Above all, you must live as citizens of heaven,
conducting yourselves in a manner worthy
of the Good News about Christ.
Then, whether I come and see you again or only hear about you,
I will know that you are standing together
with one spirit and one purpose,
fighting together for the faith, which is the Good News.

Colossians 1:28-29 NIV

He is the one we proclaim,
admonishing and teaching everyone with all wisdom,
so that we may present everyone fully mature in Christ.
To this end I strenuously contend
with all the energy Christ so powerfully works in me.

2 Timothy 1:7 NLT

For God has not given us a spirit of fear and timidity,
but of power, love, and self-discipline.

Titus 2:14 NLT

He gave his life to free us from every kind of sin,
to cleanse us, and to make us his very own people,
totally committed to doing good deeds.

1 Peter 4:8 NASB

Above all, keep fervent in your love for one another,
because love covers a multitude of sins.

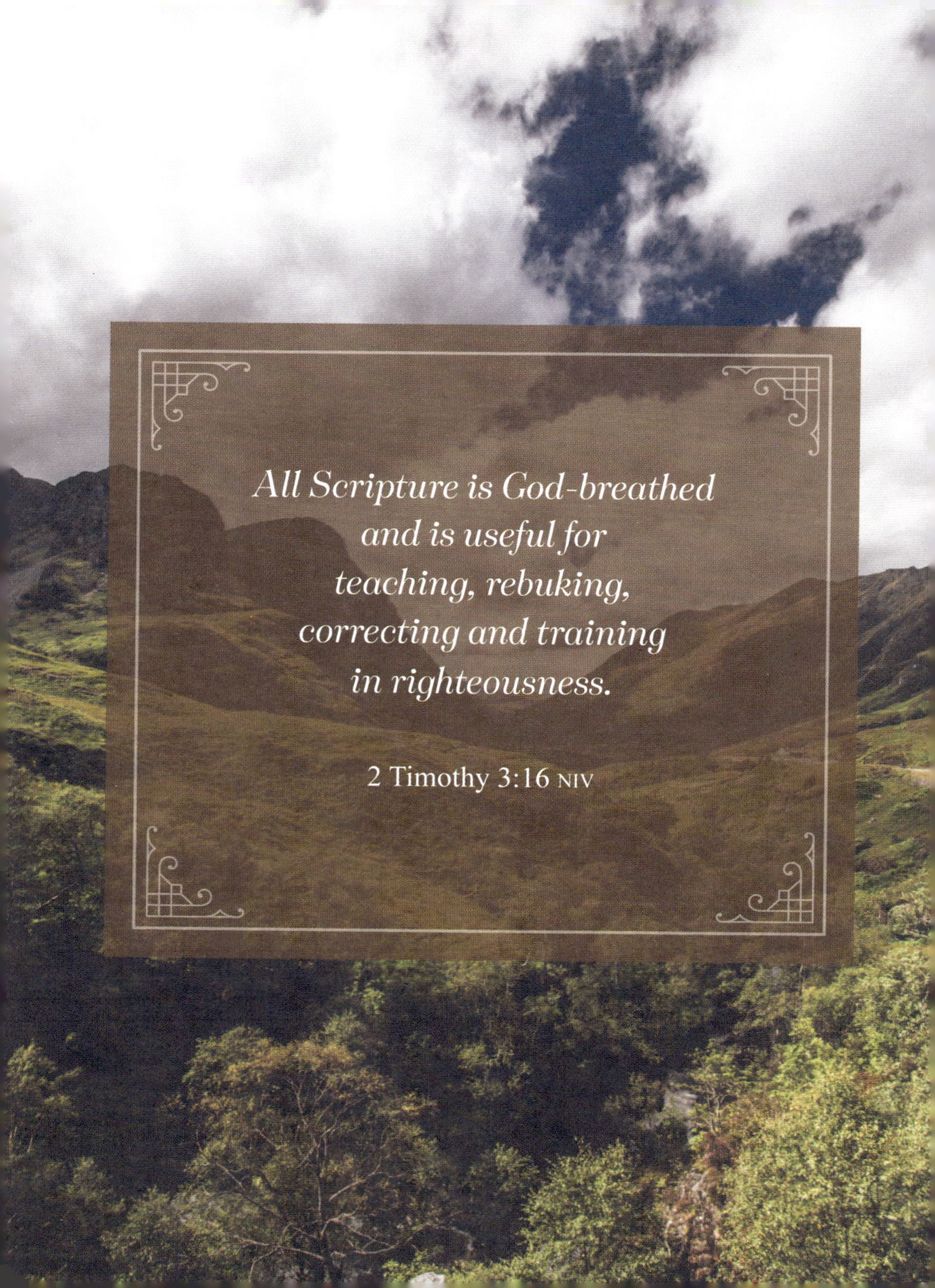
All Scripture is God-breathed
and is useful for
teaching, rebuking,
correcting and training
in righteousness.
2 Timothy 3:16 NIV

Following God by His Word

The "Word of God" can mean several things. Sometimes it is just another way of describing the Bible. God gave us the words of Scripture to tell us about Himself and to teach us how to live (2 Timothy 3:16-17). "The Word" can also refer to God's promises or to the true message about salvation. In the New Testament, we learn that Jesus is "The Word" of God (John 1). God Himself became flesh and lived among us. This is why we call Jesus the *incarnate* Word—the Word made flesh. The written Word gives testimony to the incarnate Word. We learn that, right from the start, God established the universe by His Word: "God said" and it was so. In the Psalms, the Word revealed to us in Scripture is a lamp to our feet. We do not always know exactly what the future will hold, but we are given enough light to know what step to take next. The Word has special power when it is preached since God promises that His Word will not return to Him empty but will accomplish its purpose. In 2 Timothy 3:16-17, we learn that all Scripture is "breathed out by God" and useful to the man of God for teaching, correcting and training in righteousness. We would surely be in a dark place without the precious Word of God! The student of Scripture, therefore, is not merely hoping to memorize verses for the sake of knowledge. Nor is he or she just intending to find moral instruction for daily life. We do not peruse the pages of the Bible only to have some sort of mystical experience. The goal is to pay attention to the Word of God in such a way that we hear God's voice! We must be ready to hear and eager to obey. By working through God's Word, the Spirit will enable us to follow God faithfully for His glory.

Genesis 1:3 KJV

And God said, Let there be light:
and there was light.

Psalm 119:105 NASB

Your word is a lamp to my feet
And a light to my path.

Isaiah 40:8 NLT

The grass withers and the flowers fade,
but the word of our God stands forever.

Isaiah 55:11 NASB

So will My word be which goes out of My mouth;
It will not return to Me empty,
Without accomplishing what I desire,
And without succeeding in the purpose for which I sent it.

Matthew 4:4 NIV

Jesus answered, "It is written:
'Man shall not live on bread alone,
but on every word that comes from the mouth of God.'"

Matthew 24:35 NASB

Heaven and earth will pass away,
but My words will not pass away.

1 Thessalonians 2:13 ESV

And we also thank God constantly for this,
that when you received the word of God,
which you heard from us,
you accepted it not as the word of men
but as what it really is, the word of God,
which is at work in you believers.

Hebrews 4:12 NKJV

For the word of God is living and powerful,
and sharper than any two-edged sword,
piercing even to the division of soul and spirit,
and of joints and marrow,
and is a discerner of the thoughts and intents of the heart.

*Then you will call upon me
and come and pray to me,
and I will hear you.*
Jeremiah 29:12 ESV

Following God with Prayer

There is a certain mystery to the effectiveness of prayer. *Why is it that the almighty God uses our prayers to accomplish His will?* However we slice and dice the philosophical conundrum, there is no question that God listens when we pray with a right spirit and in humility of heart. This is the clear teaching of the Bible. Nehemiah testified to this when he set out on his Herculean task of rebuilding the walls of Jerusalem. The whole project was birthed in prayer. In the prophets, God promised to renew His people through the work of the Spirit, and part of this renewal was a return to effective prayer. "Then you will call upon Me and come and pray to Me, and I will hear you" (Jeremiah 29:12). Similarly, Jesus promises that when we pray in His name, and according to His will, He will answer us (John 14:14). So it is that we are to "ask, and it will be given" (Matthew 7:7). When we are in a right relationship with God, then the prayers of a righteous person are powerful and effective (James 5:16). Core to a living relationship with our Father God is to come before Him in childlike prayer—to ask and to receive, to pray and seek and find.

Psalm 145:18 NASB

The LORD is near to all who call on Him,
To all who call on Him in truth.

Nehemiah 1:6 NIV

Let your ear be attentive and your eyes open
to hear the prayer your servant is praying before you
day and night for your servants, the people of Israel.
I confess the sins we Israelites,
including myself and my father's family,
have committed against you.

Matthew 7:7 NKJV

Ask, and it will be given to you;
seek, and you will find;
knock, and it will be opened to you.

John 14:14 NKJV

If you ask anything in My name, I will do it.

Romans 12:12 ESV

Rejoice in hope, be patient in tribulation,
be constant in prayer.

Philippians 4:6 NLT

Don't worry about anything; instead,
pray about everything.
Tell God what you need,
and thank him for all he has done.

Colossians 4:2 ESV

Continue steadfastly in prayer,
being watchful in it with thanksgiving.

James 5:16 NIV

Therefore confess your sins to each other
and pray for each other so that you may be healed.
The prayer of a righteous person is powerful and effective.

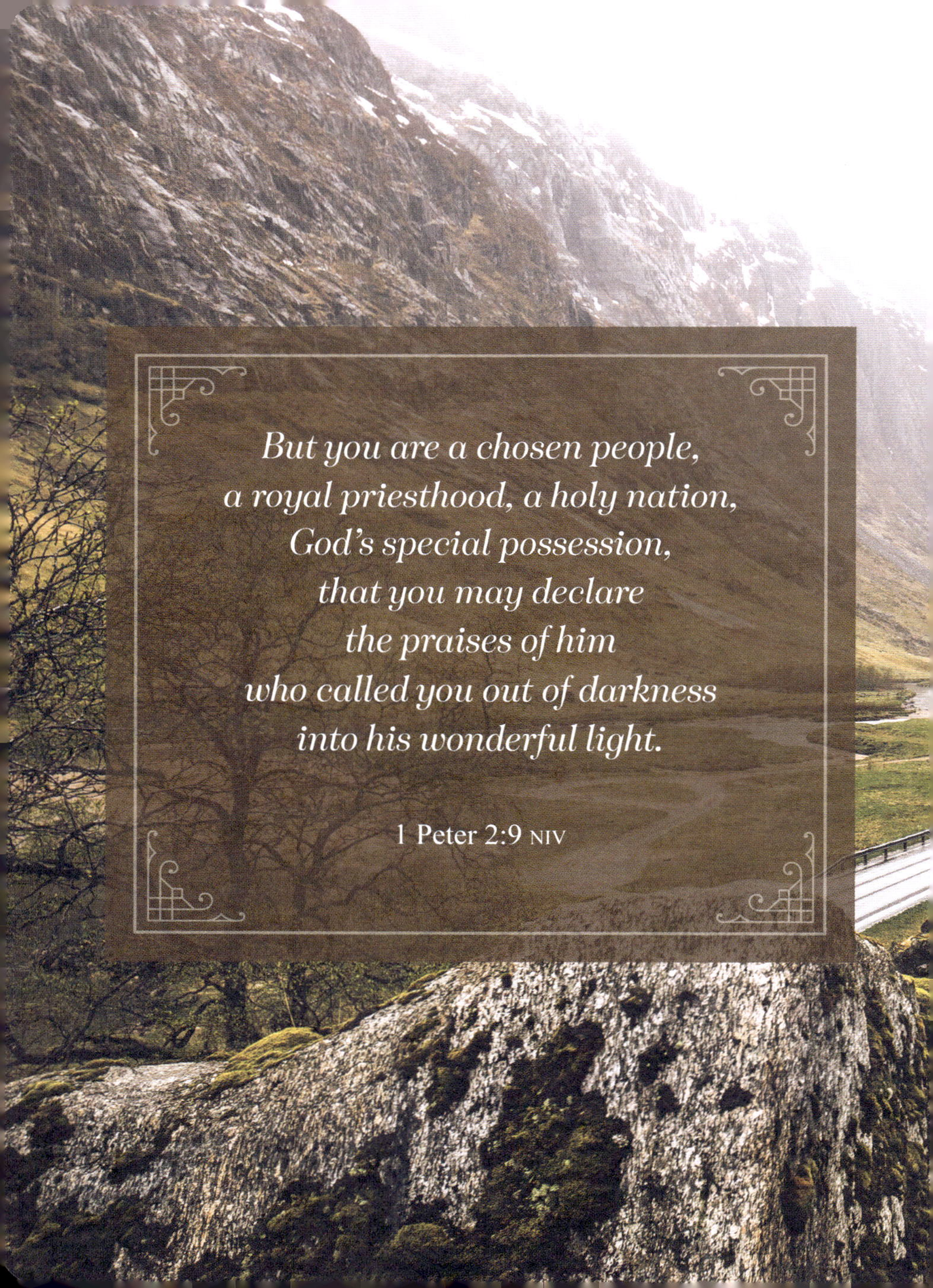
But you are a chosen people,
a royal priesthood, a holy nation,
God's special possession,
that you may declare
the praises of him
who called you out of darkness
into his wonderful light.
1 Peter 2:9 NIV

Following God with Holiness

The core idea of holiness in the Bible is of being set apart or distinct. Right from the first moment of Moses' encounter with God at the burning bush, we are told that the very ground is made holy by God's presence (Exodus 3:5). Because of God's holiness, we are therefore to be holy (Leviticus 11:45). As His people, we are to imitate Him. Our thoughts, attitudes, and actions should reflect His holiness. It is only by the power of the Holy Spirit that we can please God by our own growing holiness. Indeed, a renewed vision of God leads to a sense of how holy He is (Isaiah 6:3) and how unholy we are (Isaiah 6:5) We know that we must experience redemption and cleansing (Isaiah 6:7) ultimately through the atoning blood of Jesus (Colossians 1:20). Our practical or lived-out holiness gradually develops as we realize what God has done for us and, in gratitude and praise, we offer up our bodies as living sacrifices to serve Him (Romans 12:1). More and more, as we grow in depth of love and understanding, we realize holiness is not a negative list of *don'ts* but a positive vision of becoming who we were made to be. There is beauty in holiness, and such holiness is God's eternal purpose for us (Ephesians 1:4).

Leviticus 11:45 NASB

For I am the LORD who brought you up
from the land of Egypt, to be your God;
so you shall be holy, because I am holy.

Leviticus 20:26 NLT

You must be holy because I, the LORD, am holy.
I have set you apart from all other people to be my very own.

Psalm 139:23-24 NKJV

Search me, O God, and know my heart;
Try me, and know my anxieties;
And see if there is any wicked way in me,
And lead me in the way everlasting.

Romans 12:2 NIV

Do not conform to the pattern of this world,
but be transformed by the renewing of your mind.
Then you will be able to test and approve what God's will is—
his good, pleasing and perfect will.

2 Corinthians 7:1 NKJV

Therefore, having these promises, beloved,
let us cleanse ourselves from all filthiness of the flesh and spirit,
perfecting holiness in the fear of God.

Ephesians 1:4 NLT

Even before he made the world,
God loved us and chose us in Christ
to be holy and without fault in his eyes.

2 Timothy 2:21 NLT

If you keep yourself pure,
you will be a special utensil for honorable use.
Your life will be clean, and you will be ready
for the Master to use you for every good work.

Hebrews 12:14 NIV

Make every effort to live in peace with everyone and to be holy;
without holiness no one will see the Lord.

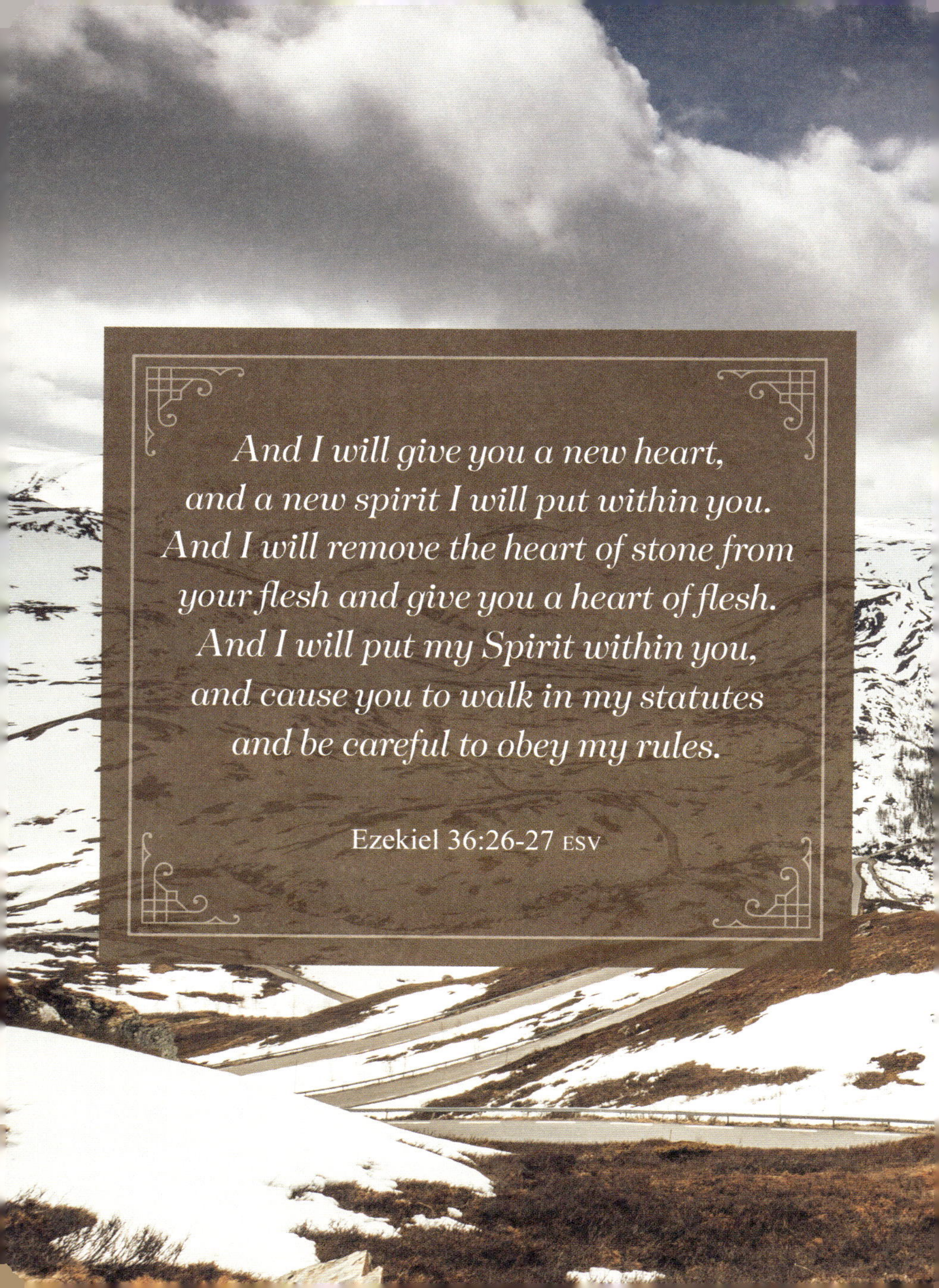
*And I will give you a new heart,
and a new spirit I will put within you.
And I will remove the heart of stone from
your flesh and give you a heart of flesh.
And I will put my Spirit within you,
and cause you to walk in my statutes
and be careful to obey my rules.*
Ezekiel 36:26-27 ESV

Following God with the Spirit

For the last hundred years or so, the work of the Holy Spirit has been mired in confusion and controversy. The key to understanding this topic, as in so much of the Christian life, is to think biblically about the work of the Spirit. The Old Testament is filled with witness to the work of the Spirit and promise of the Spirit coming in greater fullness to empower the mission of the church to all nations (Acts 2). Jesus tells us that to be saved we need to be born from above, by the Spirit (John 3). As Christians we continue to seek to be filled with the power of the Spirit so that we experience His presence and guidance and comfort more and more (Ephesians 1:13-14, 5:18, Jude 1:20-21). Jesus gave spiritual gifts to His people for their unity and edification and for the evangelization of the world (Ephesians 4:1-16; 1 Corinthians 12-14). By the power of the Spirit, God's people can effectively witness to His saving work in His kingdom (Acts 1:8). Furthermore, our holiness requires us, as Paul puts it, to "keep in step with the Spirit" and to produce the "fruit" of the Spirit: "love, joy, peace, patience, kindness, goodness, faithfulness, gentleness, and self-control" (Galatians 5). Perhaps the most beautiful picture of the Spirit's work was described by the prophet Ezekiel. Through Ezekiel, God promised His people, "I will sprinkle clean water on you, and you shall be clean... And I will give you a new heart, and a new spirit I will put within you. And I will remove the heart of stone from your flesh and give you a heart of flesh. And I will put my Spirit within you, and cause you to walk in my statutes and be careful to obey my rules. You shall dwell in the land that I gave to your fathers, and you shall be my people, and I will be your God" (Ezekiel 36:25-28).

Psalm 143:10 NLT

Teach me to do your will, for you are my God.
May your gracious Spirit lead me forward on a firm footing.

John 3:5 NASB

Jesus answered, "Truly, truly, I say to you,
unless someone is born of water and the Spirit,
he cannot enter the kingdom of God."

John 14:26 NKJV

But the Helper, the Holy Spirit,
whom the Father will send in My name,
He will teach you all things,
and bring to your remembrance all things that I said to you.

1 Corinthians 2:9-10 NLT

That is what the Scriptures mean when they say,
"No eye has seen, no ear has heard, and no mind has imagined
what God has prepared for those who love him."
But it was to us that God revealed these things by his Spirit.
For his Spirit searches out everything
and shows us God's deep secrets.

Galatians 5:22-25 NIV

But the fruit of the Spirit is
love, joy, peace, forbearance, kindness,
goodness, faithfulness, gentleness and self-control.
Against such things there is no law.
Those who belong to Christ Jesus have crucified the flesh
with its passions and desires.
Since we live by the Spirit, let us keep in step with the Spirit.

Ephesians 4:30 NKJV

And do not grieve the Holy Spirit of God,
by whom you were sealed for the day of redemption.

Titus 3:4-6 ESV

But when the goodness and loving kindness
of God our Savior appeared,
he saved us, not because of works done by us in righteousness,
but according to his own mercy, by the washing of regeneration
and renewal of the Holy Spirit,
whom he poured out on us richly
through Jesus Christ our Savior,

Jude 20-21 NIV

But you, dear friends, by building yourselves up
in your most holy faith
and praying in the Holy Spirit, keep yourselves in God's love
as you wait for the mercy of our
Lord Jesus Christ to bring you to eternal life.

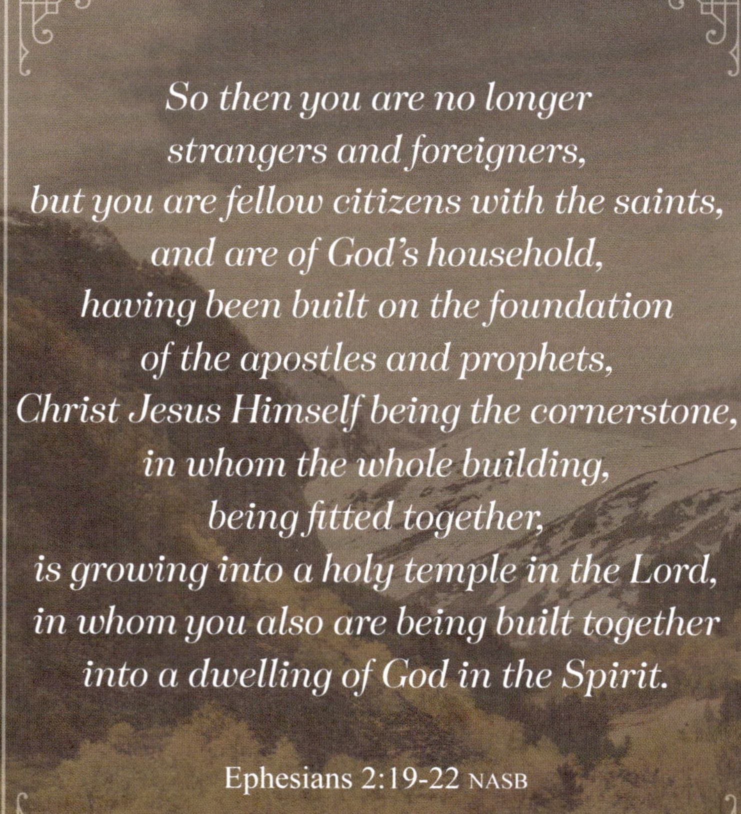
So then you are no longer
strangers and foreigners,
but you are fellow citizens with the saints,
and are of God's household,
having been built on the foundation
of the apostles and prophets,
Christ Jesus Himself being the cornerstone,
in whom the whole building,
being fitted together,
is growing into a holy temple in the Lord,
in whom you also are being built together
into a dwelling of God in the Spirit.
Ephesians 2:19-22 NASB

Following God in the Church

We live in an age whose default unit is the individual not the group, so we tend to look at all of life, including the Bible and our spiritual life, through the lens of "me, myself, and I." The Bible, though, has quite a different perspective. In the earliest days of the nation of Israel, the people gathered around the Mount of God to hear the Word of God (Deuteronomy 9:10). The translators of the Greek Old Testament described this gathering of people using the same word they used in the New Testament for "church." The assembly of God's people at the mountain was a template of what the church is today. Church is a gathering of God's people around God's Word. The New Testament reveals that the Word points to, is fulfilled by, and *is* the Lord Jesus Christ. So Jesus tells us, "I will build my church, and the gates of hell will not prevail against it" (Matthew 16:18). Wonderfully, the apostle Paul even tells the Ephesian elders that God gave His blood for the church (Acts 20:28). Jesus did not only die for us as individuals (though He surely did) but also for us as a body—a corporate unity—the church. The whole letter from Paul to the Ephesians has a strong church theme. Paul daringly says that God "put all things under his [Jesus'] feet and gave him as head over all things to the church" (Ephesians 1:22). The church is exalted in God's salvation plan. By the time we get to the book of Revelation, we are not surprised to see that it is Jesus' message to churches (Revelation 22:16). The church is Christ's bride, and it is Christ's aim to "present the church to himself in splendor, without spot or wrinkle or any such thing, that she might be holy and without blemish" (Ephesians 5:27). We may disagree about many things related to the organization of the church, but we must be clear on this—church matters.

Matthew 16:18 ESV

And I tell you, you are Peter, and on this rock I will build my church, and the gates of hell shall not prevail against it.

Acts 20:28 NLT

So guard yourselves and God's people.
Feed and shepherd God's flock—his church,
purchased with his own blood—over which the Holy Spirit has appointed you as leaders.

Romans 12:4-5 NIV

For just as each of us has one body with many members,
and these members do not all have the same function,
so in Christ we, though many, form one body,
and each member belongs to all the others.

Ephesians 1:22-23 NLT

God has put all things under the authority of Christ
and has made him head over all things for the benefit of the church.
And the church is his body; it is made full and complete by Christ,
who fills all things everywhere with himself.

Ephesians 4:15-16 NLT

Instead, we will speak the truth in love,
growing in every way more and more like Christ,
who is the head of his body, the church.
He makes the whole body fit together perfectly.
As each part does its own special work,
it helps the other parts grow,
so that the whole body is healthy
and growing and full of love.

1 Timothy 3:15 NASB

But in case I am delayed, I write so that you will
know how one should act
in the household of God, which is the church of the living God,
the pillar and support of the truth.

Hebrews 10:24-25 NKJV

And let us consider one another in order
to stir up love and good works,
not forsaking the assembling of ourselves together,
as is the manner of some,
but exhorting one another, and so much the more
as you see the Day approaching.

Revelation 22:16 NIV

I, Jesus, have sent my angel to give you
this testimony for the churches.
I am the Root and the Offspring of David,
and the bright Morning Star.

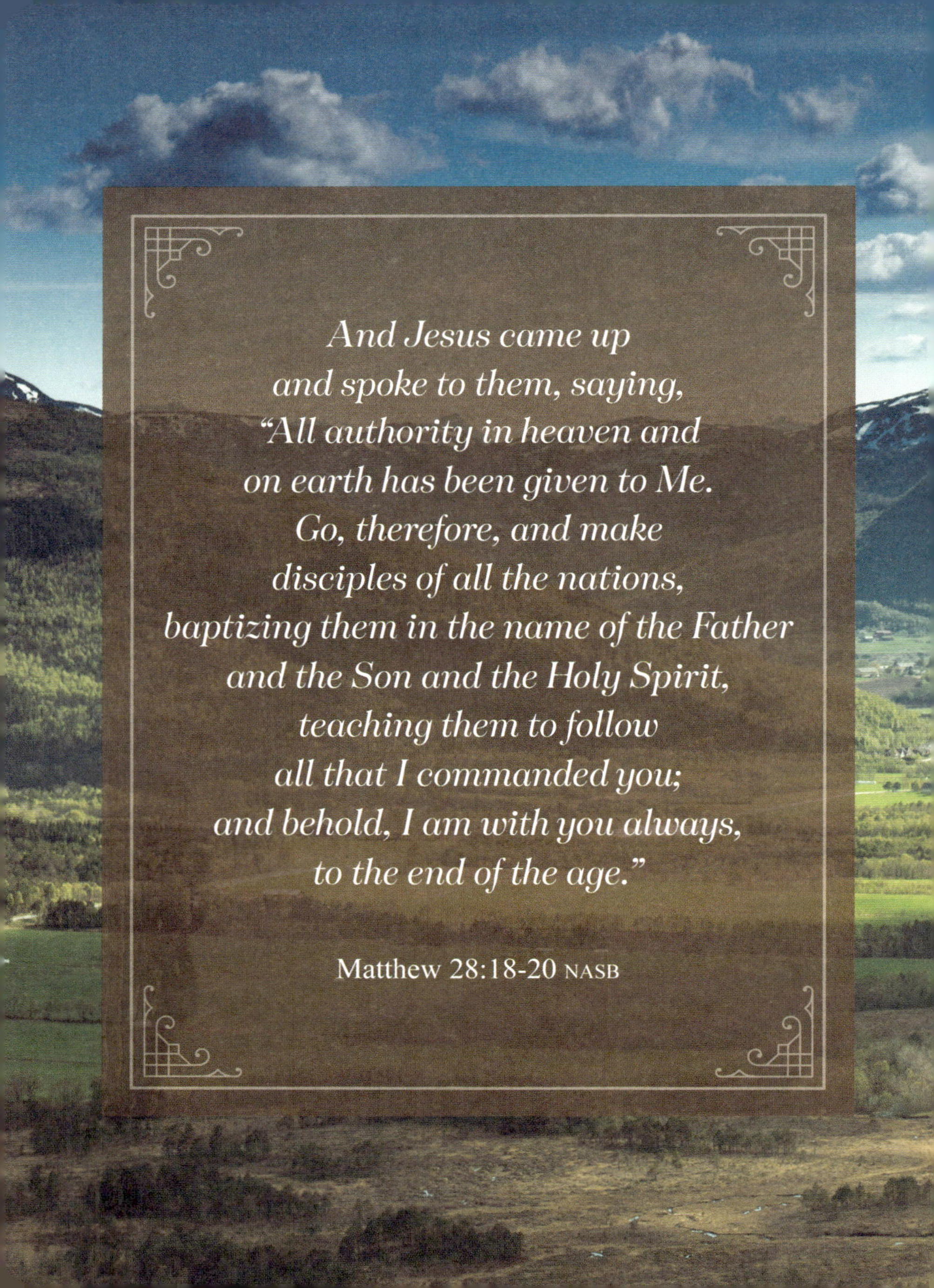
And Jesus came up
and spoke to them, saying,
"All authority in heaven and
on earth has been given to Me.
Go, therefore, and make
disciples of all the nations,
baptizing them in the name of the Father
and the Son and the Holy Spirit,
teaching them to follow
all that I commanded you;
and behold, I am with you always,
to the end of the age."
Matthew 28:18-20 NASB

Following God on Mission

It's often said that the God of the Bible is a God of mission, and therefore, God's people are on mission too. This is certainly true. From the moment when humans first rebelled against God, His mission has been to reach and reclaim the lost. But even more amazingly, and distinctively, the mission of God in the Bible is different from the "religious proselytism" so familiar to all world religions. All religions must have a constant recruitment drive, if only to keep up with the pace of population expansion. The Bible, however, does not enforce conversion (like Islam) or use false love to coerce and manipulate (like so many cults). God is a God of love, who sent "his only Son into the world, that whoever believes in him should not perish but have eternal life" (John 3:16). The mission of God is a mission of love that was shown most fully in the sacrifice of Jesus at the cross. The sacrificial love of Jesus is mirrored in the loving sacrifice of His people to reach the lost. "Evangelism" is the declaration or announcement of the earth-shattering good news of Jesus—the birth and life and death and resurrection of the God-man on our behalf. Following God on mission means that all of God's people are in a posture of readiness, knowing that we are being sent to proclaim the good news to the world around us. We know that God is sovereign, so we do not force or manipulate. We know that God's Word is powerful to save, so we declare it. We know that we must live as we speak, and so we count the cost to be those on mission too. It is the love of God that compels us.

Genesis 12:1-3 ESV

Now the Lord said to Abram, "Go from your country
and your kindred and your father's house
to the land that I will show you.
And I will make of you a great nation,
and I will bless you and make your name great,
so that you will be a blessing.
I will bless those who bless you,
and him who dishonors you I will curse,
and in you all the families of the earth shall be blessed."

Psalm 67:1-2 NIV

May God be gracious to us and bless us
and make his face shine on us—
so that your ways may be known on earth,
your salvation among all nations.

Mark 16:15-16 NIV

He said to them, "Go into all the world
and preach the gospel to all creation.
Whoever believes and is baptized will be saved,
but whoever does not believe will be condemned.

Acts 1:8 NKJV

But you shall receive power when the Holy Spirit has come upon you;
and you shall be witnesses to Me in Jerusalem,
and in all Judea and Samaria,
and to the end of the earth.

Romans 1:16 ESV

For I am not ashamed of the gospel,
for it is the power of God for salvation
to everyone who believes,
to the Jew first and also to the Greek.

Romans 10:13-14 NKJV

For "whoever calls on the name of the Lord shall be saved."
How then shall they call on Him in whom they have not believed?
And how shall they believe in Him of whom they have not heard?
And how shall they hear without a preacher?

Colossians 4:6 NASB

Your speech must always be with grace, as though seasoned with salt, so that you will know how you should respond to each person.

1 Peter 3:15 NLT

Instead, you must worship Christ as Lord of your life.
And if someone asks about your hope as a believer,
always be ready to explain it.

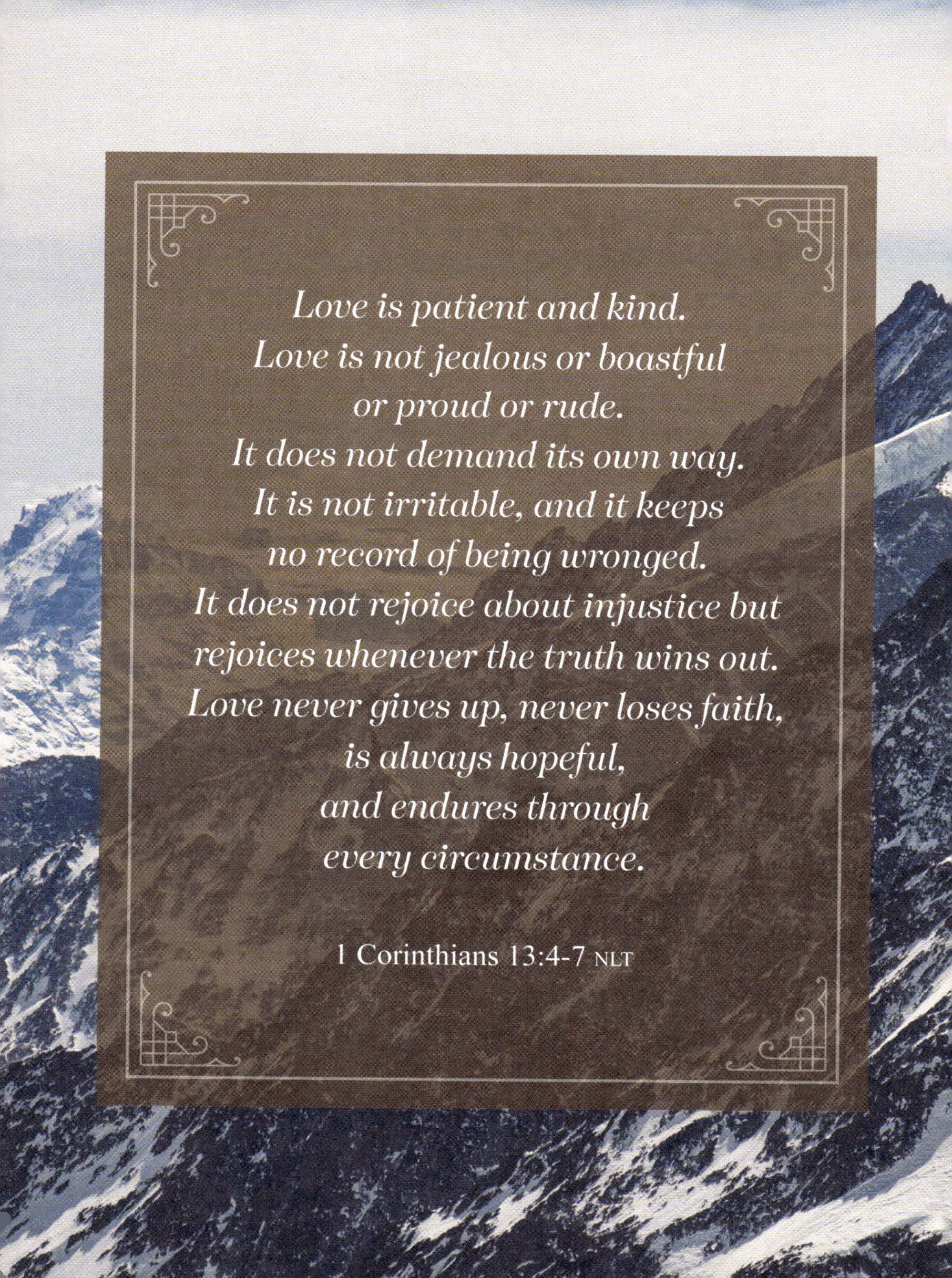
Love is patient and kind.
Love is not jealous or boastful
or proud or rude.
It does not demand its own way.
It is not irritable, and it keeps
no record of being wronged.
It does not rejoice about injustice but
rejoices whenever the truth wins out.
Love never gives up, never loses faith,
is always hopeful,
and endures through
every circumstance.
1 Corinthians 13:4-7 NLT

Following God with Love

Showing practical care, compassion, mercy, and advocacy for the least of these is part and parcel of what it means to follow Christ. According to Paul in Galatians 6:10, we as the church are to care for everyone, but particularly for each other. The teaching in the Old Testament that we are to love our neighbor is not an excuse to hate our enemies (as was being taught by the Pharisees in Jesus' time). No, we are to even love our enemies and pray for those who persecute us (Matthew 5:44). The prophets in the Old Testament similarly call us not to hide behind mere religious observance—attendance at exciting worship services or the like—as an excuse to not act in righteousness and justice. As Amos puts it, "let justice roll down like waters, and righteousness like an ever-flowing stream" (5:24 NASB). The great parable that explains how we should follow God by showing love is Jesus' story of the good Samaritan. In answer to the question *Who is our neighbor?* (that is *Who is it that we have responsibility to care for?*), Jesus brilliantly flips the question on its head by telling a story about the most unlikely person who acted neighborly. Samaritans at the time were considered religious pariahs or outcasts. But it is the Samaritan who acts as a neighbor to the person who has been robbed, while the religious leaders and others pass on by on the other side of the road. We must not only follow God in word but in deed and in truth: "Little children, let us not love in word or talk but in deed and in truth" (1 John 3:18).

Leviticus 19:18 NIV

Do not seek revenge or bear a grudge
against anyone among your people,
but love your neighbor as yourself. I am the LORD.

Proverbs 3:3-4 ESV

Let not steadfast love and faithfulness forsake you;
bind them around your neck;
write them on the tablet of your heart.
So you will find favor and good success
in the sight of God and man.

Matthew 5:44 KJV

But I say unto you, Love your enemies,
bless them that curse you, do good to them that hate you,
and pray for them which despitefully use you, and persecute you.

Romans 12:9-10 NIV

Love must be sincere.
Hate what is evil; cling to what is good.
Be devoted to one another in love.
Honor one another above yourselves.

Galatians 5:13-14 NKJV

For you, brethren, have been called to liberty;
only do not use liberty as an opportunity for the flesh,
but through love serve one another.
For all the law is fulfilled in one word, even in this:
"You shall love your neighbor as yourself."

Philippians 2:2 NLT

Then make me truly happy by agreeing
wholeheartedly with each other,
loving one another, and working together
with one mind and purpose.

1 John 3:18 ESV

Little children, let's not love with word or with tongue, but in deed and truth.

1 John 4:7-8 NIV

Dear friends, let us love one another, for love comes from God. Everyone who loves has been born of God and knows God. Whoever does not love does not know God, because God is love.

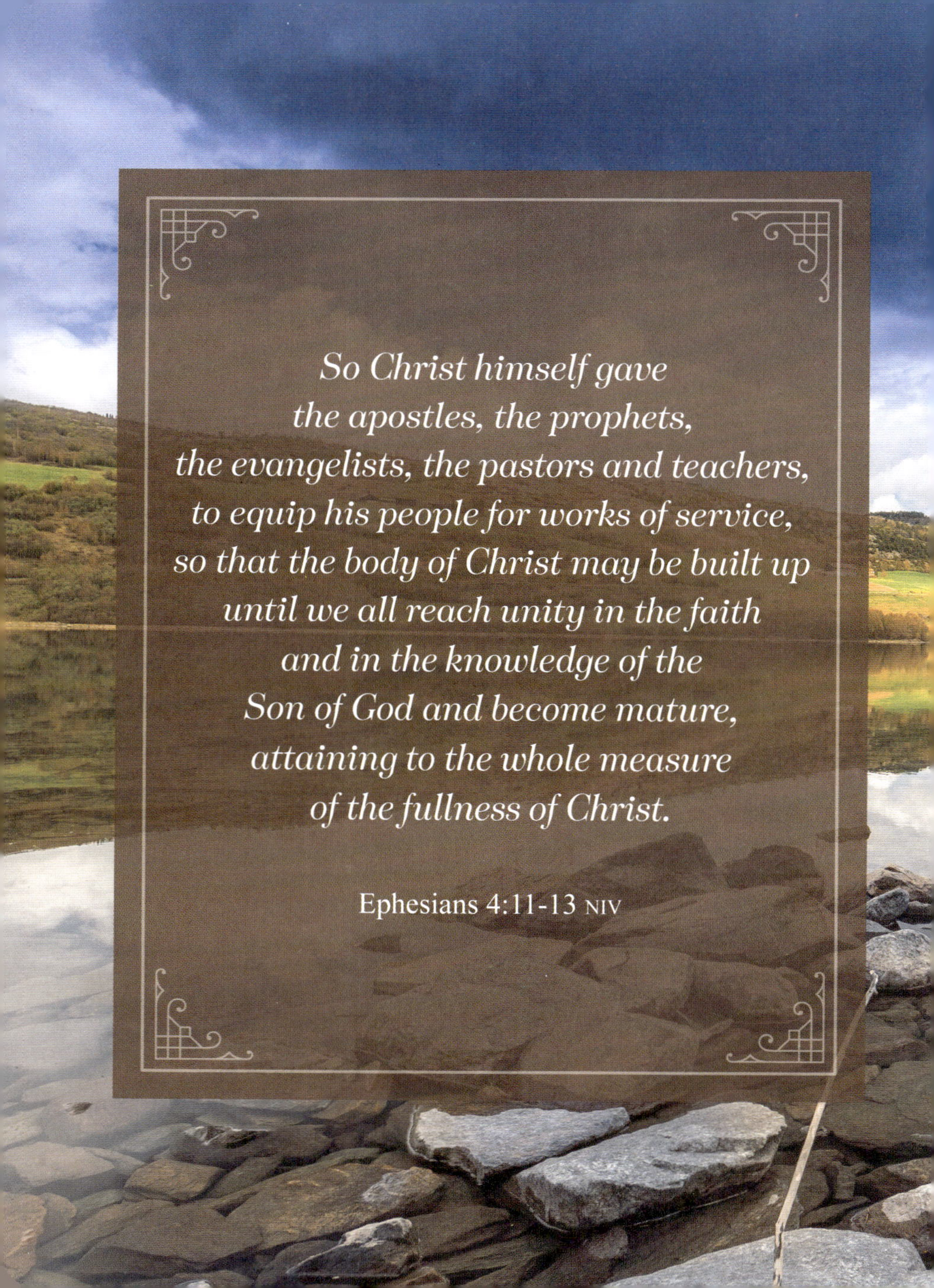

So Christ himself gave
the apostles, the prophets,
the evangelists, the pastors and teachers,
to equip his people for works of service,
so that the body of Christ may be built up
until we all reach unity in the faith
and in the knowledge of the
Son of God and become mature,
attaining to the whole measure
of the fullness of Christ.

Ephesians 4:11-13 NIV

Following God by Making Disciples

The theme of making disciples is connected to the earlier theme of following God on mission because the purpose of mission (or proclaiming the good news of Jesus) is to make disciples. However, disciple-making involves not merely the evangelization of the nations but the nurturing of Christians to full maturity. The famous text, Hebrews 6:1, encourages followers of Jesus to not be stuck in juvenile, adolescent faith but to move on to maturity. The apostle Paul was an example of someone who didn't settle for immature faith but strove forward to grow in his relationship with Christ (Philippians 3:12). This activity of being a disciple and making other disciples starts in the home. We are told in the book of Deuteronomy that it is our responsibility to disciple our children. What a difference it would make if we were as diligent at discipling our own children as the world is diligent at snatching them from the faith! This activity of disciple-making, though, goes beyond the borders of the private home or the church and reaches out to the public square—and indeed all nations—for everything belongs to Christ and is to be claimed as His through the gospel. We are to be a light to the nations (Isaiah 49:6) and salt and light for the earth (Matthew 5:13-15). A key distinctive of biblical Christianity, is an emphasis on *all* of God's people becoming mature and doing ministry (Ephesians 4:11-13). The church is not an elite group of specially gifted individuals doing everything. The church is not like a bus where one person does the driving, and all the rest go along for the ride. The church (as John Stott once put it) is more like an anthill where everyone does the work.

Proverbs 9:9 ESV

Give instruction to a wise man, and he will be still wiser;
teach a righteous man, and he will increase in learning.

Isaiah 49:6 NLT

He says, "You will do more than restore the people of Israel to me.
I will make you a light to the Gentiles,
and you will bring my salvation to the ends of the earth."

Romans 15:13 NLT

I pray that God, the source of hope,
will fill you completely with joy and peace
because you trust in him.
Then you will overflow with confident hope
through the power of the Holy Spirit.

Philippians 3:12-14 NIV

Not that I have already obtained all this,
or have already arrived at my goal,
but I press on to take hold of that for which
Christ Jesus took hold of me.
Brothers and sisters,
I do not consider myself yet to have taken hold of it.
But one thing I do: Forgetting what is behind
and straining toward what is ahead,
I press on toward the goal to win the prize
for which God has called me heavenward in Christ Jesus.

1 Timothy 6:10-11 NASB

For the love of money is a root of all sorts of evil,
and some by longing for it have wandered away from the faith
and pierced themselves with many griefs.
But flee from these things, you man of God,
and pursue righteousness, godliness, faith,
love, perseverance, and gentleness.

Hebrews 6:1 NASB

Therefore leaving the elementary teaching about the Christ,
let us press on to maturity,
not laying again a foundation of repentance
from dead works and of faith toward God.

James 1:22 KJV

But be ye doers of the word, and not hearers only,
deceiving your own selves.

2 Peter 1:5-8 NIV

For this very reason, make every effort to add to your faith goodness; and to goodness, knowledge; and to knowledge, self-control; and to self-control, perseverance; and to perseverance, godliness; and to godliness, mutual affection; and to mutual affection, love. For if you possess these qualities in increasing measure, they will keep you from being ineffective and unproductive in your knowledge of our Lord Jesus Christ.

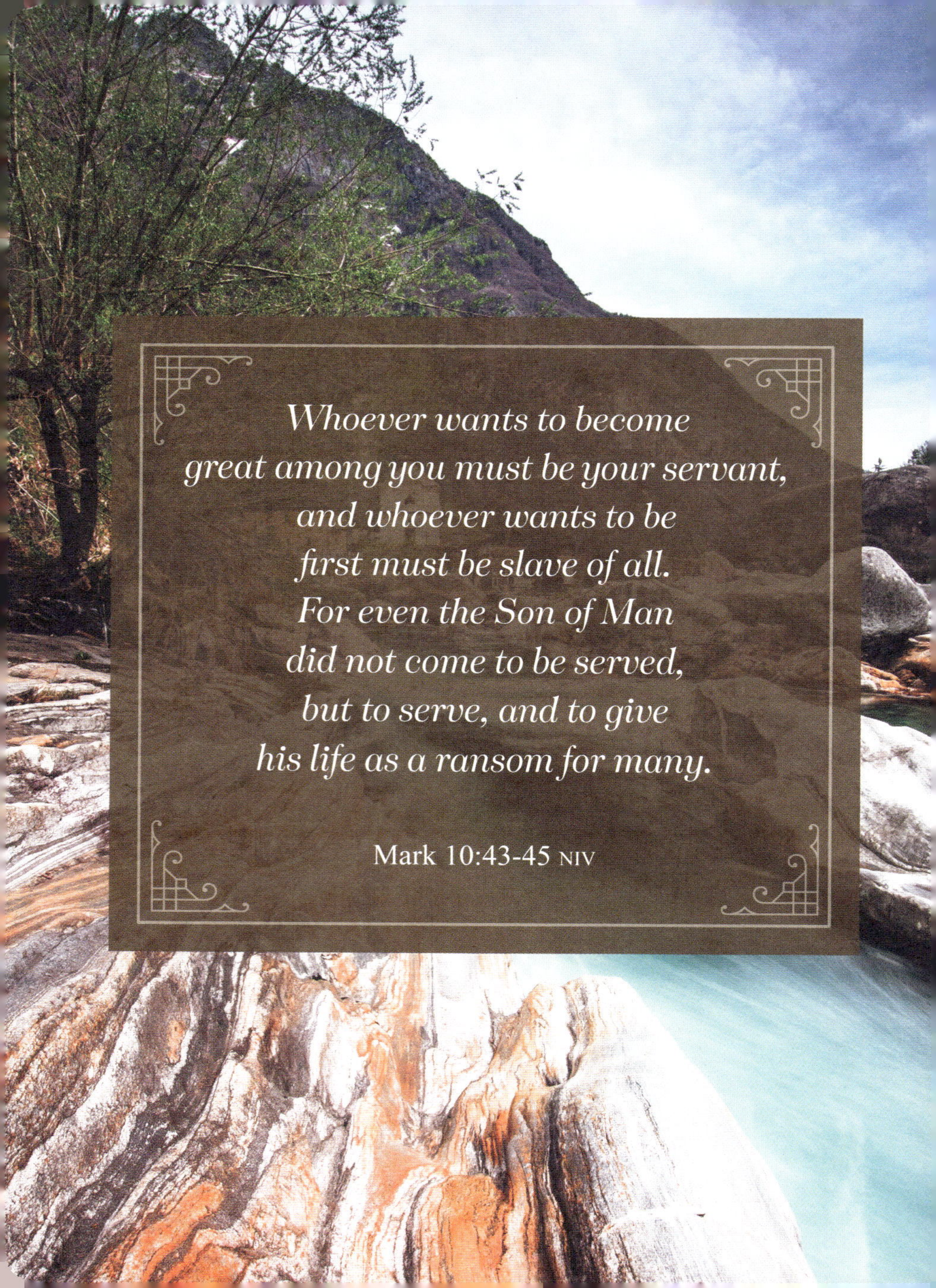
*Whoever wants to become
great among you must be your servant,
and whoever wants to be
first must be slave of all.
For even the Son of Man
did not come to be served,
but to serve, and to give
his life as a ransom for many.*
Mark 10:43-45 NIV

Following God by Serving

Followers of God are His servants—though Jesus makes it clear that we are not only servants. We are, remarkably, His "friends" (John 15:15). Our service for God is within a relational context where we are loved, valued, wanted, and cherished. It is, then, a great honor and joy to serve the Lord. We are to serve God with gladness (Psalm 100:2). This attitude of service is characteristic of the great men and women of God of the Old Testament. Moses was known as a servant of the Lord (Exodus 14:31), as was Abraham (Psalm 105:42). Wonderfully, when he first hears the voice of God calling to him, little Samuel replies, "Speak, Lord, for your servant hears" (1 Samuel 3:10). Jesus makes servanthood a core characteristic of the gospel. As He did not come to be served but to serve and give His life as a ransom for many (Mark 10:45), so we who follow Him are to serve. Those who are greatest are servants of all (Mark 10:43-44). This does not mean that we are passive toward life and the opportunities in front of us. But it does mean that we pick up the towel and serve as Jesus demonstrated when He washed His disciples' feet (John 13:14). Following God by serving means that, in view of God's mercy, we offer our bodies as living sacrifices in worship of Him. We are living sacrifices when we use the gifts that God has given us for the benefit of others and for the glory of God, not thinking of ourselves more highly than we ought, but acting on the faith that God has given us (Romans 12:3).

Joshua 24:15 NKJV

And if it seems evil to you to serve the Lord,
choose for yourselves this day whom you will serve,
whether the gods which your fathers served
that were on the other side of the River,
or the gods of the Amorites, in whose land you dwell.
But as for me and my house, we will serve the Lord.

Psalm 100:2 KJV

Serve the Lord with gladness:
come before his presence with singing.

Matthew 20:26-28 NIV

Whoever wants to become great among you must be your servant,
and whoever wants to be first must be your slave—
just as the Son of Man did not come to be served, but to serve,
and to give his life as a ransom for many.

Mark 9:35 ESV

And he sat down and called the twelve.
And he said to them, "If anyone would be first,
he must be last of all and servant of all."

John 13:14 NASB

So if I, the Lord and the Teacher, washed your feet,
you also ought to wash one another's feet.

Romans 12:3 NIV

For by the grace given me I say to every one of you:
Do not think of yourself more highly than you ought,
but rather think of yourself with sober judgment,
in accordance with the faith
God has distributed to each of you.

1 Corinthians 15:58 NASB

Therefore, my beloved brothers and sisters,
be firm, immovable,
always excelling in the work of the Lord,
knowing that your labor is not in vain in the Lord.

1 Peter 4:10 NIV

Each of you should use whatever
gift you have received to serve others,
as faithful stewards of God's grace in its various forms.

Blessed is the one who
perseveres under trial
because, having stood the test,
that person will receive the crown of life
that the Lord has promised
to those who love him.
James 1:12 NIV

Following God by Persevering

Our perseverance in the faith is grounded in God's persevering love for us. He is the kind of God who is slow to anger and abounding in steadfast love (Psalm 103:8) while also being perfectly just and righteous. The description of God in Exodus 34:6, "The Lord, the Lord, a God merciful and gracious, slow to anger, and abounding in steadfast love and faithfulness," should be read in context. The loving God is also a holy God. Yet for His people, those He has redeemed, He will and does persevere with them. We are therefore called to exercise determination and perseverance, too. If we persevere in difficult times, there will be good fruit since suffering produces perseverance, perseverance character, and character hope (Romans 5:3-4). We are called to not give up—to keep on going. The spiritual life is not like a business deal which, if we don't first get it right, we should give up and try another approach. The spiritual life is more like sowing seeds. We need to sow, and wait, and expect the seed to grow and eventually produce a harvest. "In due season we will reap, if we do not give up" (Galatians 6:9). So let us then not give up! But keep going. Let us be persistent and persevering. For we know that God will not give up on us. The righteous person falls down seven times, but seven times he gets up again (Proverbs 24:16). God has promised that He will bring to completion the good work He began in us (Philippians 1:6). The soul that has leaned on Jesus, He will not, He cannot, desert to His foes. Therefore, persevere!

Psalm 103:8 NASB

The Lord is compassionate and gracious,
Slow to anger and abounding in mercy.

Romans 5:3-4 NIV

Not only so, but we also glory in our sufferings,
because we know that suffering produces perseverance;
perseverance, character; and character, hope.

Galatians 6:9 NLT

So let's not get tired of doing what is good.
At just the right time we will reap a harvest of blessing
if we don't give up.

Philippians 1:6 NLT

And I am certain that God,
who began the good work within you,
will continue his work until it is finally finished
on the day when Christ Jesus returns.

1 Timothy 6:12 NKJV

Fight the good fight of faith,
lay hold on eternal life,
to which you were also called
and have confessed the good confession
in the presence of many witnesses.

Hebrews 10:36 NIV

You need to persevere so that when you have done the will of God,
you will receive what he has promised.

Hebrews 12:1 NIV

Therefore, since we are surrounded
by such a great cloud of witnesses,
let us throw off everything that hinders
and the sin that so easily entangles.
And let us run with perseverance the race marked out for us.

James 1:2–4 ESV

Count it all joy, my brothers, when you meet trials of various kinds,
for you know that the testing of your faith produces steadfastness.
And let steadfastness have its full effect,
that you may be perfect and complete, lacking in nothing.

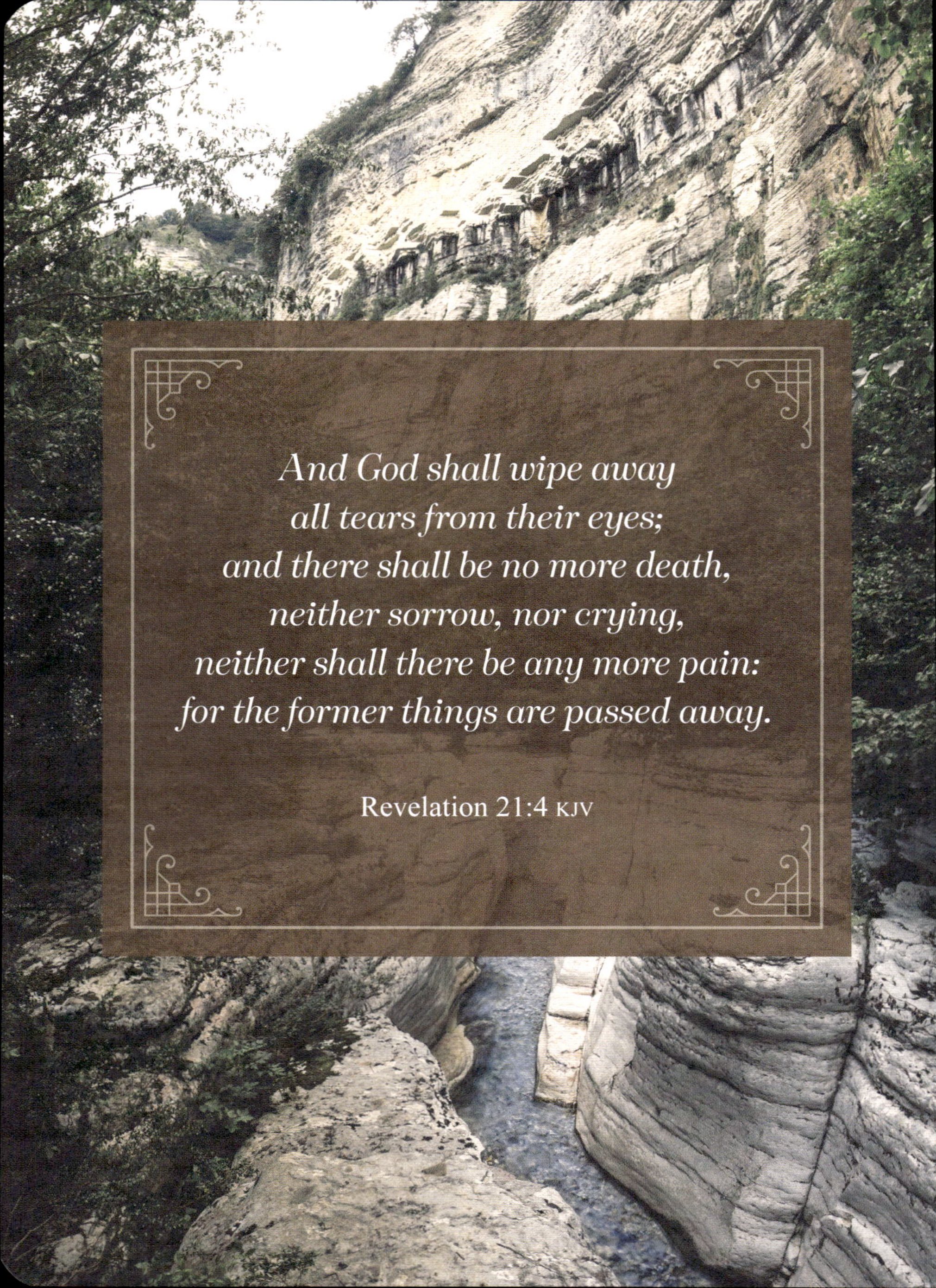
And God shall wipe away
all tears from their eyes;
and there shall be no more death,
neither sorrow, nor crying,
neither shall there be any more pain:
for the former things are passed away.
Revelation 21:4 KJV

Following God in Suffering

The so-called "problem of suffering" has troubled many tender consciences. How can a God of love allow good people to suffer? Philosophically, the answer to the question is not as difficult as often thought. After all, if God were not good, then why would we think there was anything wrong with suffering? The very question itself supposes a divine moral order with which we wrestle. We must remember also that, according to the teaching of the Bible, none of us is truly good. Every blessing—health, safety, financial provision, loving relationships, etc.—comes because God shows love and mercy to us as undeserved kindnesses. That said, at a practical level, understanding suffering is never easy. Time and time again the Old Testament book of Job describes Job's friends as giving too simplistic answers to the problem of suffering. But God clarifies that Job, though he suffered, did nothing wrong. Sometimes life is complicated. To begin to understand suffering, we must believe that several things are true. We know that God is sovereign, so in the end everything will work out for the good of those who love Him (Genesis 50:20; Romans 8:28). We also know that even though none of us are good, suffering does not necessarily occur because we have committed a particular sin. Often, suffering is a manifestation or consequence of the general rebellion of all people and the brokenness of the world. While it might not be punishment for our specific sin, suffering is still a call for people to repent—"God's megaphone to rouse a deaf world," as C. S. Lewis put it. We lament the consequences of sin and yearn for a world that is not corrupted by it. For the believer, though, there is always hope. Beyond this veil of tears, there is a far horizon where God will wipe away every tear from our eyes (Revelation 21:4). We set our hope on Him, and trust Him for the good, whether we are walking through the valley or on the heights.

Genesis 50:20 NIV

You intended to harm me, but God intended it for good
to accomplish what is now being done, the saving of many lives.

Job 42:2 NIV

I know that you can do all things;
no purpose of yours can be thwarted.

Matthew 5:10-12 NASB

Blessed are those who have been persecuted
for the sake of righteousness,
for theirs is the kingdom of heaven.
Blessed are you when people insult you and persecute you,
and falsely say all kinds of evil against you because of Me.
Rejoice and be glad,
for your reward in heaven is great;
for in this same way they persecuted
the prophets who were before you.

Luke 13:2-3 NKJV

And Jesus answered and said to them,
"Do you suppose that these Galileans
were worse sinners than all other Galileans,
because they suffered such things?
I tell you, no; but unless you repent you will all likewise perish."

Romans 8:18 NASB

For I consider that the sufferings of this present time
are not worthy to be compared
with the glory that is to be revealed to us.

Romans 8:28 ESV

And we know that for those who love God
all things work together for good,
for those who are called according to his purpose.

2 Corinthians 4:17 NLT

For our present troubles are small and won't last very long.
Yet they produce for us a glory
that vastly outweighs them and will last forever!

1 Peter 5:10 ESV

And after you have suffered a little while,
the God of all grace,
who has called you to his eternal glory in Christ,
will himself restore, confirm, strengthen and establish you.

Do not neglect to do good
and to share what you have,
for such sacrifices are pleasing to God.
Hebrews 13:16 ESV

Following God with Your Resources

The topic of money is one of those subjects that is sensitive. We tend to wonder why it is being addressed and worry that someone is trying to get something from us. Such concerns are real—deceitful salesmen do exist—but the Bible is unashamed to talk about money. It is important to remember, though, that our "resources" include far more than our material resources. In many ways, our most precious resource is that of time. We can always make more money; no one can make more time. All that we have—time, money, talents—is to be given to God. When David finished collecting donations for the temple, he prayed, "But who am I, and who are my people, that we should be able to give as generously as this? Everything comes from you, and we have given you only what comes from your hand" (1 Chronicles 29:14 NIV). Giving our resources to God reminds us how much we've been given, and it increases our gratitude. Furthermore, generosity with our resources tends toward happiness, and someone who gives freely tends to be filled with cheerfulness (2 Corinthians 9:7). This might make generosity seem self-interested, but being motivated by our own joy is not wrong—we were made to rejoice in that which is good and, ultimately, in the One who is good—God. Indeed, once we've experienced the joy of giving, we do need to be urged to pursue a life of generosity as Paul urged the Corinthians (2 Corinthians 8–9). God loves a cheerful giver who gives not under compulsion, but for joy and for God's glory.

Proverbs 11:24 NIV

One person gives freely, yet gains even more;
another withholds unduly, but comes to poverty.

Proverbs 22:9 NKJV

He who has a generous eye will be blessed,
For he gives of his bread to the poor.

Luke 16:13 NIV

No one can serve two masters.
Either you will hate the one and love the other,
or you will be devoted to the one and despise the other.
You cannot serve both God and money.

2 Corinthians 9:7 NIV

Each of you should give what you have decided in your heart to give,
not reluctantly or under compulsion,
for God loves a cheerful giver.

2 Corinthians 9:11 NLT

Yes, you will be enriched in every way
so that you can always be generous.
And when we take your gifts to those who need them,
they will thank God.

Galatians 6:10 NKJV

Therefore, as we have opportunity, let us do good to all,
especially to those who are of the household of faith.

James 2:15-16 NIV

Suppose a brother or a sister is without clothes and daily food.
If one of you says to them, "Go in peace; keep warm and well fed,"
but does nothing about their physical needs, what good is it?

1 John 3:17 NKJV

But whoever has this world's goods,
and sees his brother in need,
and shuts up his heart from him,
how does the love of God abide in him?

About the Author

Josh Moody (PhD, University of Cambridge) serves as the senior pastor of College Church in Wheaton, Illinois. He is also the president and founder of God Centered Life Ministries. Josh is an expository preacher who seeks to bring God's Word into the practical matters of the human condition and heart. Josh and his wife Rochelle have four children.

Notes

Notes